Praise for *Rhythm*

"*Rhythm* changed our entire business. In the first year, we had a $3.5M turn-around that was the direct result of becoming more focused and aligning our resources. This is only our second year and the process continues to have an exponential impact on our company. Rhythm has been the single most important investment we've made in the last twenty-three years."

—Randy Carr, president and CEO of World Emblem International, Inc.

"Complexity is a byproduct of growth, and without proper attention to the right priorities, future growth will likely stall. Patrick helped us define those priorities that are truly driving our business forward making energy and resource allocation simple."

—Mike Rans, vice president and general manager of Kinkelder USA

"*Rhythm* is a very readable, practical guide for what entrepreneurs and CEOs can do to meet growth challenges and grow successfully. I'm particularly pleased that Thean recognizes the importance of strengthening teams as they grow and finding other jobs in the company for people who have maxed out. I'd recommend this book to every entrepreneur, CEO, and senior manager in a company with growth potential."

—Brad Smart, bestselling author of *Topgrading*

"Growth is an imperative for high-potential ventures, and the acceleration of growth comes from excellence in execution. Thean has an acute understanding of this paradigm but he advances that thinking by introducing rhythm as a conceptual imperative for a growing company. *Rhythm* leverages thought, planning, and execution competencies to increase value. If you think you have a good company, read this book and you might make a lot more money than you ever conceived possible."

—Stephen Spinelli, Jr., PhD, cofounder of Jiffy Lube; president of Philadelphia University; former vice provost of entrepreneurship and global management at Babson College, and author of seven business books

"*Rhythm* introduced me to a new system to enhance harmony and balance in our companies. It's about hitting that sweet spot between the tense times and the safe times in the growth cycle for every company."

—Jack Stack, CEO of SRC Holdings Corp and
author of *The Great Game of Business*

"The rhythm of business is accelerating and the nature of strategy is transforming. Thean offers a tested, proven process for winning in a fast-paced world."

—Kaihan Krippendorff, CEO of Outthinker LLC
and author of *Outthink the Competition*

"If you want to lead a great company, Patrick Thean has written the how-to on achieving greatness. The system he has designed works! Design the future, put the plan together to realize your future, then implement with impeccable discipline. This is the framework for the ultimate success story. The process works—Arbill is living proof."

—Julie Copeland, president and CEO of Arbill, and chair of the
Women's Business Enterprise National Council Forum (2014–2015)

RHYTHM

HOW TO ACHIEVE
BREAKTHROUGH EXECUTION
and ACCELERATE GROWTH

PATRICK THEAN

GREENLEAF
BOOK GROUP PRESS

Published by Greenleaf Book Group Press
Austin, Texas
www.gbgpress.com

Distributed by Greenleaf Book Group LLC

For ordering information or special discounts for bulk purchases,
please contact Greenleaf Book Group LLC at PO Box 91869,
Austin, TX 78709, 512.891.6100.

Design and composition by Greenleaf Book Group LLC
Cover design by Greenleaf Book Group LLC
Cover image: ©iStockphoto.com/Maydaymayday

Rhythm® is a registered trademark of Patrick Thean and Leadline, LLC.
Think Rhythm™; Plan Rhythm™; Do Rhythm™; Think Plan Do Rhythm™;
SuperGreen™; and Red-Yellow-Green™ are trademarks of Patrick Thean and
Leadline, LLC.

Publisher's Cataloging-In-Publication Data
Thean, Patrick.
  Rhythm : how to achieve breakthrough execution and accelerate growth /
Patrick Thean. — 1st ed.
    p. ; cm.
  Includes index.
  Issued also as an ebook.
  ISBN: 978-1-62634-079-4
  1. Organizational change. 2. Business planning. 3. Management. 4. Success
in business. I. Title.
HD2746 .T44 2014
658.4/06   2013954839

Part of the Tree Neutral® program, which offsets the number of
trees consumed in the production and printing of this book by
taking proactive steps, such as planting trees in direct proportion to
the number of trees used: www.treeneutral.com

Printed in China on acid-free paper

18 19 20 21 22 23 10 9 8 7 6 5 4

First Edition

To my parents,
Who instilled in me the values of hard work,
determination, and integrity.
Thank you for your unconditional love and support.

CONTENTS

PART 3: DO RHYTHM   175

ACKNOWLEDGMENTS

This book could not have been written and finished without the help of my colleagues and customers. I first want to thank Cindy Praeger who encouraged me to keep going every time I felt that the book had conquered me and it was too much to do. Your ability to keep the end in mind while encouraging me to rewrite just one more time is astounding. Your dedication and commitment are greatly appreciated. I also want to thank Lari Bishop, my editor. This book could not have been birthed without Cindy and Lari.

I want to thank my Dream Team at Rhythm Systems. Jessica Hoffpauir proofread this book numerous times. Thank you for being meticulous. Ryan Walcott, Chris Cosper, Nancy Sacani, Tiffany Chepul, Barry Pruitt, Alan Gehringer, Melissa Enriquez, Deb Colson, Melissa Perna, Jennifer LeVine, and Ray Wee. How you guys found time to help me and review the work while taking care of our customers was amazing. Thank you for your involvement, support, and passion. It is truly a blessing to be able to work with each one of you every day.

I also want to thank Verne Harnish, who has dedicated his life to helping entrepreneurs and growth companies. Thank you for the impact you have had on my professional life. As the founder of YEO (Young Entrepreneurs Organization) now called EO, you have helped so many entrepreneurs. Your teachings—*Mastering The Rockefeller Habits*, *The One Page Strategic Plan*, and *Meeting Rhythms*—have inspired a lot of my work.

God has blessed me with an amazing family. You don't get to choose your family; God chooses them for you. Thank you Lord for my parents. I am deeply indebted to my amazing wife, Pei-Yee. Your love and selfless dedication to Joy, Nicole, and me is what allows me to thrive at home and at work.

Last but not least, thank you to our clients. It is a privilege to work with each of you. Thank you for trusting us with your teams and your dreams. Special mention goes to the following clients who shared their stories and specific insights about how they broke through their ceilings of complexity—those growth challenges that can stop any company in its upward climb. Nothing helps us learn better than real-life stories and examples. Thank you for sharing how you used Rhythm to grow your business and get your teams focused, aligned, and accountable, so that other entrepreneurs can learn from your experiences and apply it to their own situations.

Hostopia: Hostopia is a leading provider of private-label web services and business-communication tools. For over a decade, Hostopia has collaborated with the most successful companies in the worlds of telecommunications, media, and retail to activate new sales channels and generate new revenue streams. Before being sold at a premium of 2.3 times the publicly traded valuation, Hostopia was run by Colin Campbell, one of the founders of the company. Hostopia now operates as a subsidiary of Deluxe Corp. www.hostopia.com

AvidXchange: Run by cofounder and CEO Michael Praeger, AvidXchange revolutionizes the way leading companies across industries pay their bills through automated invoice and bill payment processing. Not only are the teams at AvidXchange experts with over ten years of experience automating companies' bill payment processing, they are also pioneers who were first in their industry to automate invoice processing. www.avidxchange.com

Chicago Public Schools: Chicago Public Schools is the third largest school district in the United States. Within this district, the

Office of School Improvement (OSI) works to better conditions for Chicago's students who are most vulnerable to school dropout and lifelong poverty. The mission of OSI is to radically and quickly transform Chicago's most struggling schools through effective implementation of federally sponsored school-wide reform initiatives. OSI was built under the leadership of Donald Fraynd, now the founder and CEO of TeacherMatch. www.cps.edu

TeacherMatch: is a company founded by a group of dedicated, passionate educators who understand that *teachers are the most critical factor* in student learning. In concert with their team of top academics, they have taken a groundbreaking step forward in advancing the quantitative and scientific aspects of hiring. Using cutting-edge predictive analytics on teaching effectiveness, their revolutionary platform predicts the impact of teacher candidates on student achievement and identifies the top candidates for any position schools need to advance learning. Their mission is to measurably increase student achievement and elevate the teaching profession by placing more effective, higher-quality teachers in all classrooms through the use of predictive analytics. www.teachermatch.org

MobilityWorks: MobilityWorks is a national chain of certified wheelchair-accessible van providers. They have more than twenty showrooms across the country, and offer a large selection of wheelchair vans and assistance from a staff of trained experts to better meet the needs of their customers. Their business is divided into two units: the consumer division, which consists of retail locations, and the commercial division, which serves public transportation providers like taxi services. The company is led by Bill Koeblitz, President. www.mobilityworks.com

Dutch Valley Food Distributors: Dutch Valley Food Distributors is a wholesale bulk-food distributor to a variety of retail outlets in twenty-nine states under the leadership of CEO Matt Burkholder. Dutch Valley has been committed to its mission to "bring honor and glory to God by pursuing the highest standards of excellence and integrity, putting relationships first and engaging in successful commerce" since 1978. With the environmental and economic advantages of bulk foods, Dutch Valley Foods has grown from about twenty employees to over two hundred. www.dutchvalleyfoods.com

White Lodging: White Lodging, founded by Bruce White, is a leader in development and management of premium-brand hotels. Their portfolio includes over 170 mid- to large-scale hotels, including iconic brands like Marriott, Sheraton, and Renaissance, and almost thirty restaurants across the country. White Lodging employs over six thousand associates through their Hospitality Management Division, run by Dave Sibley, President and CEO of that division. Bruce White remains the Executive Chairman of the White Lodging Group. www.whitelodging.com

Simms Fishing: Simms is the number-one choice of fly fishermen, especially professional guides, for apparel and gear. Innovators in their field, Simms Fishing was one of the first companies worldwide to introduce neoprene waders to provide waterproofing and warmth to serious anglers. Their unique breathable product was developed through their exclusive partnership with W. L. Gore & Associates (makers of GORE-TEX fabric). They remain dedicated to producing the highest-quality products for all fishing conditions and are committed to manufacturing their products in the United States. K. C. Walsh, President, leads the company and its 130 employees at their headquarters and production plant in Bozeman, Montana. www.simmsfishing.com

BioPlus Specialty Pharmacy: BioPlus is a national, award-winning specialty pharmacy, currently providing pharmaceutical care to more than three thousand patients. BioPlus has the skilled people and innovative technology to make it easy to refer and measurably improve the outcomes of patients facing complex chronic health conditions, such as bleeding disorders, hepatitis C, cancer, Crohn's disease, and rheumatoid arthritis. BioPlus is led by CEO and founder Dr. Stephen Vogt. www.bioplusrx.com

Veeam: Veeam is a leader in virtual machine (VM) backup. They specialize in fully leveraging the virtual environment to provide VM backup at reduced cost and increased value to more than eighty thousand customers worldwide. This rapidly growing international company develops innovative products for virtual infrastructure and data protection under the leadership of Ratmir Timashev, President and CEO. www.veeam.com

ImageFIRST: One of the largest and fastest-growing companies to provide laundry services to outpatient medical facilities around the country, ImageFIRST has been in business for over forty years and has thirty-six locations and over three hundred employees. They have maintained one of the highest customer retention rates in their industry and exceed the industry standards of excellence under the leadership of Jeffrey Berstein, President. www.imagefirst.com

"Jack" or "Jill": I use the names "Jack" or "Jill" to protect clients or friends as I share their experiences for your learning pleasure. These stories are all lessons learned from real business leaders. If you are one of my friends and identify too closely with a story, then it might just be about you—or another CEO who faced a similar challenge. If you think it might be you, I thank you for the insights you've shared that may help other entrepreneurs or business owners or leaders achieve their goals and change the world.

BREAKTHROUGH EXECUTION

*That's been one of my mantras—focus and
simplicity. Simple can be harder than complex.
You have to work hard to get your thinking clean
to make it simple. But it's worth it in the end because
once you get there, you can move mountains.*

—Steve Jobs

When Colin Campbell invited me to help him at Hostopia, the company was bringing in about $22 million in revenue with a couple hundred employees. They had recently gone public, raising about $30 million on the Toronto Stock Exchange. Colin and his brother Bill had done what they had set out to do: grow this company successfully.

That may sound like a dream come true to you. And it was for Colin. However, all of that success came with a new level of complexity for the business, and new problems Colin was struggling to solve. He and Bill were serial entrepreneurs and Hostopia was their fourth company. "You'd think I would be having fewer headaches and making more money with a company this successful," he said to me. "Things seem more complicated than they should be." Colin wasn't quite sure what changes he needed to make, but he knew that what had worked before was no longer working.

The biggest sign that he needed to do something different was that revenue growth had begun to falter. They had grown rapidly for the previous five or six years. But since going public, their growth rate had fallen to below 20 percent—lower than shareholder, analyst, and board expectations. They weren't hitting their forecasts quarter after quarter. The result? Colin and his team felt blindsided when their financial results were reported and their stock price went down instead of up.

Decision making had slowed down, too. "Great ideas are being bounced around, but not in a formalized way, so we aren't making progress," Colin said, and then he described how that was affecting the fast-growth culture they had built early on. "Employees who have been with the company for a while are telling me that things aren't like they used to be. My energy and belief in the company used to pull the team forward. Now we have over three hundred employees in offices all over the world. We're struggling to get everybody on the same page." The company was lacking a clear strategy for continued growth that every employee understood, and the slower response time wasn't helping.

As Colin shared his concerns, it became apparent to me that Hostopia had hit a ceiling of complexity, particularly in their ability to execute as a team. It had become much more difficult to choose the right priorities. Not choosing well meant the team was less aligned, and competing priorities were fighting for the same resources. They felt as though they were taking one step back while taking two steps forward. Data from different divisions were telling them to take action. But there were too many things to do and not enough time, people, or resources. They were less confident in their choices about what actions to take. Things appeared okay on the surface and to the rest of the world, but the leaders knew that the company was not working as well as it had before. They did not know how to navigate past certain challenges of growth, people, and operations. They felt stuck. I felt for Colin and his team. But I also knew that their problems were not unique.

All growth companies encounter ceilings of complexity, usually when they hit certain milestones—fifty employees, one hundred employees, $15 million in revenue, $100 million in revenue. These tipping points vary based on the types of businesses we run, our past experiences, and the growth rate of our firms. *When* we hit them may be different for each of us. But what is certain is that we *will* hit them. And when it happens, suddenly what we used to do doesn't work anymore. The left hand doesn't seem to know what the right hand is doing. This first occurs with little things. We might even make jokes and laugh at ourselves. Then, before we know it, these small misalignments accelerate and we become like the slower companies we were making fun of the week before. I still recall the day at my own company when a newly hired employee walked by my office and I asked my partner Ray, "Who is that?" Ray looked at me in surprise and said, "What? You don't remember? We hired him for R&D last month!" Ouch!

Colin's situation reminded me of a time when I was feeling the same pressures, and what I fondly recall as my "Jerry Maguire moment." I remember it that way because in the movie, Jerry Maguire hit a crisis point, woke up at two a.m., and changed his life from that point on. At the time of my moment, I was running a company called Metasys, a transportation-logistics software company that I had founded in 1991. Metasys was a rocket ship—growing at 100 percent a year, hitting 151 on the Inc. 500 list in 1996, accumulating Fortune 500 clients, attracting top project-management talent from the best consulting firms. It was exhilarating and stressful.

One night, I woke up at two a.m. in a cold sweat. My gut told me that we were headed for a train wreck. But how could that be? We had done everything right: top talent, weekly project status meetings, financial metrics tracked and on target. Part of me said that I should dismiss the feeling and go back to sleep. After all, the experienced and talented individuals in my company were handling everything better than I could. Right? I was wide awake and my heart was pounding. I finally had to get up and work on proving my gut right or wrong.

Our data and metrics were all measuring the past. So I started asking a different set of questions—questions about how to identify train wrecks in the making and how to track those signs and make adjustments to avoid being blindsided.

Never dismiss your gut just because other, more experienced people tell you everything is okay. Your gut is the best leading indicator you have.

That night, I had an epiphany. My epiphany was that our data and metrics were all measuring the past. So I started asking a different set of questions—questions about how to identify train wrecks in the making and how to track those signs and make adjustments to avoid being blindsided. These were future-focused questions. And over time, those questions led to a bigger revelation: To be a future-focused company and avoid being blindsided by opportunities and threats, we had to spend time on a regular basis thinking about the business, planning our execution, and doing the work necessary to get us to where we wanted to be.

We needed a rhythm to continually identify the right things to review and discuss in order to help us stay focused on the future and avoid being blindsided. And once we found it, this rhythm propelled us forward, past ceiling after ceiling of complexity.

Once Colin was all talked out, I reminded him that he had built a strong company. And he should celebrate that! Too often, we type A personalities don't pause and celebrate our victories. We just look for the next problem to solve. But like any other successful company, all Hostopia needed was an approach that would ensure long-term growth and help Colin make the right decisions and give him the confidence to execute with single-minded focus and commitment. Colin needed to implement three key rhythms.

3 Key Rhythms to Execute Well

1. **Think Rhythm:** A rhythm of strategic thinking to create focus for the future of your business

2. **Plan Rhythm:** A rhythm of execution planning to let all teams and individuals know what they are supposed to do

3. **Do Rhythm:** A rhythm of doing the work to keep the plan on track

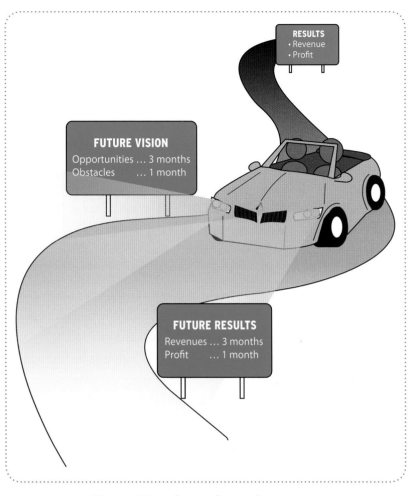

Figure 1. Be a future-focused company.

So Colin and Hostopia started using these three rhythms to get their teams at all levels of the company focused, aligned, and accountable. I met with Colin and his team for two days every quarter as part of their Think and Plan Rhythms. They met every week as part of their Think and Do Rhythms. They started solving problems quickly, they moved past their ceiling of complexity, and they started having fun again.

The right rhythms give you focus, alignment, and accountability.

Less than two years after we started working together, Hostopia was purchased by Deluxe Corporation for 17 times EBIDTA, which was equal to 2.3 times their current public valuation! Most companies sell for less than 10 times EBIDTA. If they are public companies, they get purchased at a valuation slightly above their publicly traded value; 2.3 times their current public valuation is a significant premium. But possibly the most validating part of the sale was a meeting that Colin had with the CEO of Deluxe Corporation and his management team. Colin described Hostopia as a professionally managed organization. He described their Think, Plan, and Do Rhythms. He showed them how Hostopia had a culture that was focused, aligned, and accountable for delivering results. At the end of his presentation, the CEO of Deluxe Corporation, a much larger company, turned to his team and said, "Guys, this is what I'm talking about. This is the kind of intensity and focus that we need to bring to our company." Then he told Colin that Hostopia had the framework and foundation to become a $500 million company.

The Power of Think, Plan, and Do Rhythms

The best thing about having Think, Plan, Do Rhythms is that they make you and your organization continuously ready to deal with ceilings of complexity when you meet them. When you hit a ceiling of complexity, you should not have to start up new processes and new habits to help your teams deal with change. In fact, making smart adjustments in your organization as part of the three rhythms helps you avoid hitting those ceilings completely. Don't waste money and time redesigning your company for each stage of growth. Your rhythms should ensure that your teams are ready to respond, learn, and improve *as you grow*.

The Rhythm Systems Rhythm Team has helped clients all over the world get their teams focused, aligned, and accountable by implementing the Think, Plan, Do Rhythms. Having done thousands of sessions for clients on five continents, missing only Africa and Antarctica, we have gained unique insight into the most important patterns and tools that help companies grow. I'm excited to share them with you in this book. The most important lesson, though, is that successful companies have the three rhythms in place. They have a Think Rhythm—a rhythm of strategic thinking to keep their teams focused, working on the future of their business. They have a Plan Rhythm—a rhythm of execution planning to choose the right priorities and get

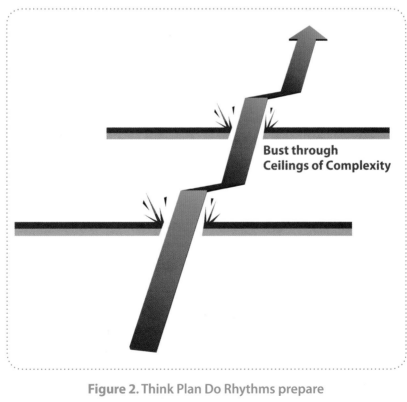

Figure 2. Think Plan Do Rhythms prepare
you to make smart adjustments.

their departments or divisions aligned. And they have a Do Rhythm—a rhythm of executing the plan and making effective and timely adjustments every week.

These are the rhythms necessary to grow, and to grow with purpose. No aspect of your business goes unexamined for very long when you have these rhythms in place. You don't drift toward success or failure. Every goal, every action, helps you achieve your purpose, week by week, quarter by quarter, year by year.

The Think, Plan, Do Rhythms aren't linear. They are all in force at the same time. Every week, you spend time on strategic thinking. Every week, you are planning your execution for the coming week. Every week, you are doing the work and making adjustments. These are strong, regular, and repeated patterns of organizational behavior, not just a process for solving a particular problem.

You might be asking, "What is the difference between a rhythm and a process?" Great question. A process is a series of steps designed to help you accomplish something consistently. For example, a customer-issue-resolution process is a series of steps from A to Z to resolve customer complaints or concerns. A rhythm is a habit that repeats, allowing you to be proactive and innovate when the need arises. Let me emphasize that: A rhythm allows you to be proactive. You need both rhythms and processes to be successful. For example, if you have a rhythm of reviewing customer support calls, it might lead you to identify customer issues that have not escalated yet into full-blown crises. Once customer issues have been identified, you can develop the right process to solve it.

Fire prevention instead of firefighting! The Think, Plan, Do Rhythms allow you to make critical adjustments early in response to obstacles or challenges coming your way. And that's how you blow past ceilings of complexity.

Fire prevention instead of firefighting! The Think, Plan, Do Rhythms allow you to make critical adjustments early in response to obstacles or challenges coming your way. And that's how you blow past ceilings of complexity.

How This Book Will Help You Develop Rhythm and Grow

If you have hit a growth ceiling and find it difficult to achieve sales the way you used to, you might not be sure what to do. Look at it as a blessing; it's a problem faced only by growing companies. If you are stagnant, you will not have to worry about hitting any ceilings of complexity! The key is not to avoid it, but rather to prepare for it. Consider now the demands that growth will place on your organization in the future. Are you prepared for the growth you want? Is your execution strong enough?

You can read this book from start to finish, or you can jump to the discussions of particular rhythms, depending on your need.

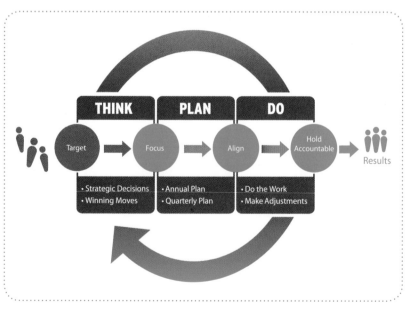

Figure 3. Think, Plan, and Do Rhythms

Part 1: Think Rhythm

The Think Rhythm is about working on the future of your business through strategic thinking. It offers three benefits: First, it helps you strengthen your foundation for future growth. Second, it ensures that you have a continuous supply of winning moves to provide purposeful revenue growth. Third, it helps your teams focus on what to do annually, quarterly, and weekly to advance your winning moves. You'll learn how to

→ Develop a Think Rhythm that puts strategic thinking in your flight path every week, every quarter, and every year.

→ Identify aspects of your core business that could be tightened to ensure sustainable growth.

→ Choose and work on the right winning moves. These winning moves should provide you with growth to double your revenue over the next three to five years.

→ Understand the opportunity costs of losing moves that steal your energy, time, and resources. Then get rid of those moves!

Part 2: Plan Rhythm

The Plan Rhythm is about execution planning that helps teams and individuals understand what they are supposed to do. It requires figuring out the company priorities that will drive your strategy forward, and then making sure that every single person understands and is aligned with those priorities. Every year and every quarter, you have an opportunity to create a vision that energizes your teams to achieve a goal. And if you back up the vision with metrics and tracking tools, everyone will know how they're progressing and if they need to make adjustments. Each quarter provides you with thirteen weeks to move your strategy forward. Empower your teams to run a thirteen-week race. The chapters in part 2 will help you

→ Implement a Plan Rhythm that helps you energize your teams and align them to achieve specific goals every year and every quarter.

→ Learn how to discuss, debate, and agree so that you can focus on the right priorities.

→ Cascade your execution plan to align all teams in your company.

→ Identify the right success criteria for each priority so that you can hold your teams accountable and make adjustments to succeed.

Part 3: Do Rhythm

The Do Rhythm is your process of getting work done and executing your plan. By being accountable to your execution plan, you can discover which critical adjustments need to be made and brainstorm options and opportunities. When we make adjustments proactively, we achieve our goals faster. The chapters in part 3 will help you

→ Develop a Do Rhythm that helps people stay focused on priorities; and

→ Build a habit of reviewing data and insights weekly to make necessary adjustments.

I will end with a story of a customer who has been applying Rhythm for the last seven years. It is really cool to have a macro view of the progress and results over the last seven years. It shows you how to put all these things together in a few pages! And when you do, you will find that your company will be well prepared to execute for growth. More important, you will enjoy your journey.

Throughout the chapters, look for Rhythm Expert Tips. The Rhythm Systems Rhythm Coaches have helped many companies develop the rhythms I'll describe in this book. Their valuable expert advice may help you progress faster.

At the end of each part, I will also share my Rhythm Action Items—essential first steps to implementing and leveraging rhythm in your organization.

To help you get started, I'm offering a free assessment at www .PatrickThean.com. Take the assessment now and at least once a year. Throughout the book, I will also provide tools, worksheets, and exercises to make integrating rhythm into your organization as simple as possible. (These tools are available for free download on the website. Check back occasionally for the latest versions and improvements.) The most important thing, though, is that you take the first step.

Change Works Best One Step at a Time

I have seen too many CEOs and company executives get excited about what they learned at a conference, come home to a week or two of brilliance, and then fade back into the old status quo. What happened? Well, an event happened. But change and improvement do not evolve from events. Our most successful clients document a simple path of progress (POP), allowing them to focus on a few things versus many things. The POP unburdens you from feeling like you have to get to every improvement immediately. Instead, it gives you confidence as you plan a path forward, focusing on a few things at a time. I asked Colin Campbell what advice he would share with other leaders of companies, and he said, "I would caution leaders to commit to the process completely, but take it one step at a time. Focus on doing one thing, get it right, then start working on something else."

I wrote this book to change the world by enabling company owners and entrepreneurs to achieve their dreams, one step at a time. I hope you find this book helpful as you set out to grow your firm. I also hope that you will write to me (at Patrick@Thean.com) and share the stories of your successes.

Enjoy your progress and your journey, and thank you for reading my book.

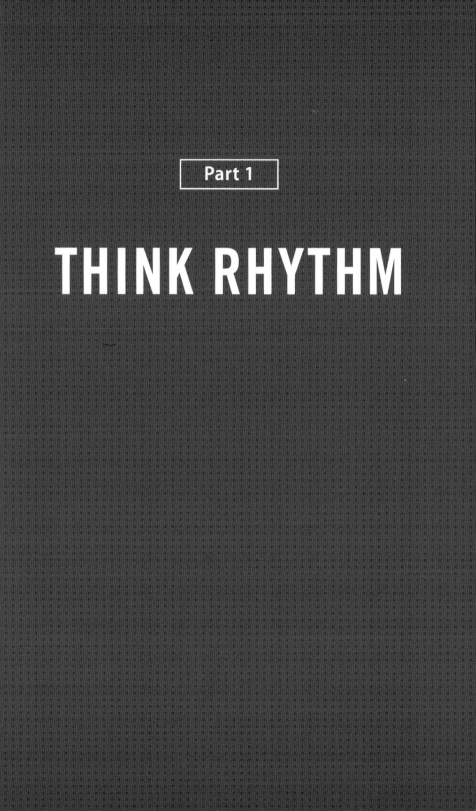

Part 1

THINK RHYTHM

CHAPTER 1

THE SECRET TO GROWTH IS DEVELOPING A HABIT TO THINK

It is not enough to have a good mind;
the main thing is to use it well.

—René Descartes

In January 2012, a company called AvidXchange celebrated a major event: a single online bill payment. Doesn't sound like much, right? You—or your bank—probably make online bill payments every month. You go to the online bill-paying system for your account, enter payment and payee information, and ta-da, you've paid your bill online!

While it is easy for an individual or consumer to make a payment online, it is harder than you might think for a business to pay their vendors electronically. Unlike individuals, businesses have to make sure that payments are integrated into their accounting systems, that the right people have approved the invoice, that payment is sent to vendors in a form they can receive. It can be a complex process for some companies, so it took years of thinking and planning for AvidXchange to launch an online bill-payment system for businesses. It was a move that put them on a path to double their business in fifteen months. I call these high-growth moves *winning moves*.

I had been working with AvidXchange since 2001, when the company was just a year old. Today, it is a fast-growing software-as-a-service (SaaS) company with revenues north of $30 million. They built the company on the concept of paperless accounts-payable automation, and their flagship product was called AvidInvoice.

By 2010, AvidXchange had become a leader in accounts-payable automation in the real estate industry. But like any hot technology company, their first-to-market advantage wasn't going to last forever. While they were still at the top of their game, they needed to identify the next winning move to fuel their growth and stay ahead of the competition. They could tell that a growth ceiling was looming. Rather than wait until revenue started to flatten, they began the process to find their next winning moves.

In 2001, the AvidXchange team had committed themselves to a strong and regular rhythm of getting together for two days every year and every quarter and spending time thinking about how to grow the business. And every week, they met for an hour to share and discuss any feedback that they might have received from prospects and customers regarding their products and services. They used this feedback to fine-tune their offerings and improved their ideas and products week after week, quarter after quarter.

This rhythm allowed them to work on new winning moves ahead of time. After many sessions, they realized that they had an internal asset that they could monetize. They had relationships with their business clients and their customers' vendors. These vendor relationships were created as they helped their customers validate vendor invoices. And they had already integrated their solution with customers' accounting systems. This combination made AvidXchange uniquely qualified to provide an online bill-pay system for businesses. This was a winning move that could potentially double the company revenue in two years, and even 10X it in the long term!

I can't emphasize enough the value of this kind of rhythm. We would like to think that success happens overnight, that winning moves appear overnight, but they don't. The lesson we can learn from AvidXchange is that it takes the habit of spending time—on a regular and consistent basis—working on and refining your strategy to create success. I call this a Think Rhythm.

We would like to think that success happens overnight, that winning moves appear overnight, but they don't.

Think Rhythm: Put Thinking Time in Your Flight Path

Most executives I ask would agree that it is important to spend time thinking strategically about the future of their businesses. Yet most leadership teams fail to do so. They fail because they do not have a clear and simple way to get this strategic thinking time into their company routine or regular flight path.

Take a closer look at your regular day. What does it look like? Is it filled with various meetings and customer deliverables? Maybe a fire to put out here and there? No leader is sitting on his or her butt waiting for something strategic to do! Being busy with the day-to-day operations of the business is the most common excuse I hear from executives for not having time to think and work on winning moves. Then a few years down the road, their growth flatlines. They are left scrambling desperately for growth. As a CEO or executive, you are accountable for the growth of your company. Provide a clear path to that growth instead of scrambling to try to birth a winning move overnight. "We don't have time" really means that a strategy for growth was not important enough. It did not make the short list. If you truly believe that it *is* important, prioritize it above the other things that compete for your time. Put a Think Rhythm into your flight path!

"We don't have time" really means that a strategy for growth was not important enough.

RHYTHM EXPERT TIP

Be proactive about scheduling time to work on your strategy and the future growth of your business. Schedule a weekly lunch meeting with your team and focus only on strategy.

Michael Praeger, the CEO of AvidXchange, said to me, "The best advice you ever gave me was to take two days every quarter and every year, get out of my company, and work on the business. It has turned

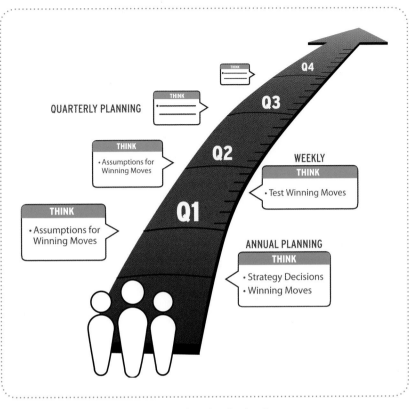

Figure 4. The Think Rhythm

out to be one of the best habits we have today. We do this every quarter and year, regardless of our current situation. We spend that time working on the future of our business and planning exactly what we are going to achieve as a team for the upcoming quarter. In twelve years, we have never missed a session, and they have been amazing. Over the years, this rhythm forced us to stop and think when we least wanted to or when we thought we couldn't afford the time. We kept to our rhythm and met anyway. Ironically, those were the times when we needed to stop and think the most. This rhythm has allowed us to head off a number of crises and develop a vision and strategy for our future."

[Our Think Rhythm] forced us to stop and think when we least wanted to. . . . Ironically, those were the times that we needed to stop and think the most.

Not only did the Think Rhythm help AvidXchange develop a game-changing winning move, it has also helped the team beat their competition to become a leader in electronic invoicing. In 1999, one of their competitors raised $200 million in capital, compared to AvidXchange's $1.5 million. I remember discussing the competitor's war chest in a Think Rhythm meeting. Michael was wondering how they could compete with their tiny $1.5 million. Imagine that—going to war against a competitor with 133 times more capital than you! I helped Michael and his team focus on what they could affect, and they built a strategy based on e-invoicing for a single industry. They worked on that strategy every quarter. Ultimately the competitor with the massive war chest couldn't compete against AvidXchange's focus and discipline. The competitor flamed out during the dot-com bust. AvidXchange rode it out. In fact, they've repeated this victory time and time again, most recently with their winning move of becoming an e-payment company.

Implement this Think Rhythm in your company today if you want to ensure your future:

→ **Two-day annual and quarterly sessions:** The first day is part of your Think Rhythm. Spend time working on the future of your business. Work on systematically developing winning moves and building your foundation to make sure you are able to grow with purpose. The second day is part of your Plan Rhythm, which I will cover in part 2.

→ **Weekly talk and think time:** Spend at least an hour every week pushing your strategies forward. In his book *Good to Great*, Jim Collins provided a great process he calls The Council.

Yes, the Think Rhythm includes meeting quarterly *and* weekly. If you want to achieve breakthroughs in your growth, you have to keep moving your strategies forward. If you put strategic thinking on hold between quarterly or annual Rhythm sessions, you won't successfully execute your strategy. I'll explain winning moves in more detail in the rest of part 1, but know that you should be testing your ideas before you pour your full resources into executing them. You should be collecting real-world data, observing customer reactions, and talking about your findings with your executive team. Don't be afraid of obstacles. Confront them and solve them. The obstacles were already there. You did not create them. The faster you uncover them, the faster you can bust through them and succeed! Use your Think Rhythm to uncover them quickly and find solutions.

I recently facilitated a company's annual strategy and execution–planning session. I had also facilitated their last annual session. As we reviewed their strategy, the lack of real-world data and insights made it clear that they had not made progress. They had not spent time thinking and working on their winning moves over the last twelve months. This company's leadership team was too focused on their day jobs and had not invested time to test and validate their strategy. When I shared this insight with them, they realized that they had to get on a regular Think Rhythm to work on their strategies and winning moves before another twelve months flew by. They were still inspired by their plan. That's wonderful. Inspiration is good, but inspiration coupled with perspiration is much better!

What should you spend time on during these Think Rhythm sessions? Two things: Work on and improve the foundation of your company when necessary, and develop winning moves to drive revenues and growth.

Building a Strong Foundation to Scale

Ratmir Timashev, CEO of Veeam, was facing a unique situation when

I first started working with him and his team. Veeam is a global software company that builds solutions for managing virtual backup and replication. Veeam had no problems growing revenue. In fact, they were experiencing hypergrowth. "We grew from ten million to over a hundred million very fast. It took us five years. And our goal in the next five years is to hit one billion." How many companies hit $1 billion in their first ten years? Very, very few. And it can be incredibly stressful if you stumble or hit a few roadblocks. Those roadblocks can cause a bunch of fires that need to be put out. How do you navigate hypergrowth while preventing fires instead of firefighting? Let me show you how Veeam used a Think Rhythm to thrive during their hypergrowth.

Hypergrowth is a mixed blessing. Maintaining profitability and strong execution becomes a big challenge.

Ratmir was very clear about why he needed my help. He wanted to make sure that his company was ready to maintain good execution and profitability as their revenues zoomed past $100 million. Hypergrowth is a mixed blessing. Maintaining profitability and strong execution becomes a big challenge. He was being proactive to ensure that they could avoid stumbling blocks that could spoil their positive momentum.

"Most of us don't have experience leading a company that's over a hundred million," Ratmir told me. *Not many leaders do*, I thought. "We are in unknown territory. To grow is one thing, but to stay profitable and continue with our fast growth is another." Veeam had a very focused growth strategy with a few winning moves. They were being proactive, ensuring that the strategy could be executed well and that it would lead to the growth they predicted. This would help them avoid the ceilings of complexity that slow most companies down.

I helped the Veeam management team establish a Think Rhythm to review key strategy elements that are important to all growth companies. These included their core purpose, core values, BHAG®[1] (Big Hairy Audacious Goal, as defined in Jim Collins's book *Built to Last*), core customer, brand promise, and winning moves. We did not work on all of these items at once. Instead, we got on a path of progress and worked on them one at a time. Over the next year, with the discipline of a quarterly Think Rhythm, monthly coaching discussions, and weekly meetings, Veeam reviewed and fine-tuned their strategy elements and maintained their growth momentum.

For instance, reviewing their core customer definition helped them to examine how their resources were being deployed to service customers. They were devoting resources to multiple market segments, from large enterprise organizations to small to mid-sized businesses (SMBs). This was beginning to be stressful as these two types of companies had very different business requirements for their software.

A common mistake is for companies to think about the market segments that they are in instead of understanding the person who really uses their products and services. We live in a P2P world—a people-to-people world. And it is the people who work for companies—not the companies themselves—that buy your products and services. Companies don't buy anything. Only humans do! So what does that person look like? What does he or she need? This core customer may exist in more than one market segment. Veeam discovered that their core customer did in fact exist more and more in the

....
1   BHAG is a registered trademark of Jim Collins and Jerry Poras.

enterprise segment, even though originally most of them lived in the SMB segment. This insight helped them focus their growth strategies on servicing their core customer. And it improved their focus on those few winning moves that were most likely to get them to the $1 billion goal.

"We assumed that we were all thinking or behaving the same way, even on the executive management team," Ratmir said.

Over the next year, the executive team used their Think Rhythm to systematically examine and refine their core values and clarify their BHAG. I would facilitate and work with them during their two-day quarterly sessions to refine key strategy elements on their path of progress. Then over the next three months, the senior team would continue making progress with Tiffany Chepul, their Rhythm coach. We would then confirm their decisions at the next quarterly session, and begin work on the next thing. When they were ready, they rolled out these foundational elements to the whole company. Sharing their strategy in this way allowed them to align more than a thousand employees as they continued to navigate hypergrowth. This is how they are scaling the business past $100 million in a controlled way.

Clarifying and communicating the elements of your strategy gives you a strong foundation to scale your company. These foundational elements permeate all operational priorities. They are long-term decisions that serve as guideposts so that when you're trailblazing, you don't lose your way. They are domino decisions—when you make one of these decisions, it translates into one hundred other decisions. They allow employees to make the right decisions. They allow you to recruit well. They help you execute winning moves efficiently. Great winning moves should be aligned with all aspects of your strategy. They must serve the needs of your core customers, allow you to grow with purpose, and take you closer to your BHAG. You have to be intentional about these decisions because they define your path forward.

Be proactive and review your foundation at every annual session. Get all of your strategic elements on a single page. Not only does it make discussions easier, but it also allows you to effectively communicate these elements throughout the company and execute with alignment throughout the year. I use the One Page Strategic Plan developed by Verne Harnish and described in his book *Mastering the Rockefeller Habits*. It is a beautiful, simple, and powerful tool—one page to capture all of your strategic elements and your execution plans. It is easily shared, posted, referenced, and used. At your annual meeting, pull out your One Page Strategic Plan and talk about anything that may have changed about your company or the market that requires an adjustment. Here are some questions that might help you review elements of your foundation during your annual meeting:

→ Does our behavior show that we are living our core values? Have we hired or fired anyone based on our core values?

→ Are we clear on our long-term goal? Do we have a vision for what we would like to achieve in the next three years? Five years? Ten years? Are we making decisions with our BHAG in mind? Are our actions taking us closer to or further away from it?

→ Are we building products and services that our core customers need?

→ Are we taking on projects that help fulfill our purpose?

→ Are our people able to make key decisions without asking permission because they know how to use our purpose and core values?

→ On the operational side, have we envisioned what our company will actually look like if we achieve our vision for the next three, five, and ten years? How many employees will we need? What will our annual growth rates look like? How might our leadership structure need to be adjusted?

If you haven't figured out these crucial pieces of your company, create a path of progress to work on them one at a time. Clarify and confirm the foundation of your strategy, and you will be able to grow efficiently and with purpose.

Dr. Stephen Vogt, CEO of BioPlus, understands the power of purpose. He has used it to build a strong team and a strong company. When he contacted us, he said, "We are a pretty good company, but I want us to get better and stronger." Truly great companies are always trying to get better. BioPlus's core strategic elements—their purpose, core values, and brand promise—were so clear and strong, the team had an incredible foundation from which to grow to greatness.

BioPlus is a national specialty pharmacy that deals in medications for chronic, complex, and life-threatening conditions, such as cancer, bleeding disorders, immune system disorders, Crohn's disease, rheumatoid arthritis, and hepatitis C. They help maximize patient outcomes by customizing their processes for each physician, therapy, and patient. Dr. V. shared BioPlus's brand promise: "BioPlus makes it easy to admit a specialty pharmaceutical patient and ensures an optimum outcome. To ensure an optimum outcome, we help them adhere to the medication orders and help the patient to never miss a dose." They pride themselves on their high-touch approach, which helps ensure that patients comply with their medication regimens. The treatments they specialize in take months, have nasty potential side effects, and *cannot be interrupted.* We were discussing the hepatitis C therapy and I asked, "What if the treatment gets delayed by a couple of days?" Dr. V. explained: "Each dose the patient misses increases the likelihood of a resistance to the medicine occurring and thus a failure in the treatment. Studies have shown this. We spend much time educating the patient that we will do whatever it takes to get them their medicine, if they will do whatever it takes to complete the course of therapy without interruption." Uncured, these patients will likely develop cirrhosis, which can lead to liver failure or liver cancer. BioPlus made certain that their patients adhered to and completed their treatment, an effort aligned with the company's purpose: "To enrich the lives of our patients and customers and energize our employees to do so."

A patient we'll call "Grace" and Hurricane Sandy would test Bio-Plus's commitment to their promise and purpose.

Grace had been diagnosed with hepatitis C twelve weeks before Hurricane Sandy hit the northeastern United States. She had received the hepatitis C virus during a blood transfusion two decades before. Two weeks after starting her treatment, the side effects hit and hit hard. She developed a rash and bleeding hemorrhoids, and a fiery itch covered her body. She suffered through mouth sores and extreme dry skin. At the six-week point of her treatment, she received fantastic news. A blood test verified that the virus was undetected in her body. If she just endured the side effects a little longer and finished her treatment, she was likely to be cured!

Grace's next batch of treatment was being rushed to her as Hurricane Sandy was approaching the New Jersey shore. Unfortunately, Sandy got there first, making landfall not far from Grace's home. Her medication was stuck in a distribution center in another state.

For Grace, it was a good thing that BioPlus was serious about their brand promise and purpose. They were monitoring Grace's medication and the storm. They knew that she needed her medication by Friday. They had only days to keep their promise. Clearly they needed a Plan B.

Dr. Nick Maroulis, director of pharmacy at BioPlus, told me that they worked as a team to develop and implement various solutions for getting the medication to Grace.

Plan B: They contacted numerous hospitals to see if there were any medication samples that she could use as a stopgap. No nearby doctors had any samples.

Plan C: Then they tried to transfer Grace's prescription to a local pharmacy. This plan created the risk of them losing Grace as a patient to another pharmacy. "But it is more important to us that a patient does not miss a single dose," Nick said. They were unable to find a local pharmacy with the medication.

Plan D: Finally, as they were running out of time, Nick's team packed a fresh batch of refrigerated medication and chartered a private jet to fly it to Grace. The jet landed in New Jersey on Friday morning, the package was picked up by a private courier, and the courier delivered it to Grace in the hurricane-devastated area at nine a.m. Grace injected herself with the medication within an hour of the scheduled time.

BioPlus kept their promise. Grace did not miss a single dose. Nick concluded that the adjustment they made with Plan D was the right thing to do. "Chartering a private jet was pretty expensive and unique, but every day here at BioPlus we go the extra mile for patient compliance; chartering a plane was just an extension of that philosophy."

The most remarkable part of this case study was that these decisions were made without consulting Dr. V. The team understood that enriching patient lives and keeping their promise of "never missing a dose" was of the utmost importance. Dr. V. uses a Think Rhythm to review BioPlus's strategy with his team on a regular basis. He keeps what's important to the company top of mind by communicating the company's strategy with his team on a regular rhythm.

Dr. V. has built a pretty special company, one in which the team acts to enrich lives without the fear of repercussions. He has built a culture that encourages people to confidently and quickly take the right actions. "At BioPlus," he told me, "you cannot make a mistake as long as you make decisions using our core values and focus on our purpose. There may be less expensive ways to do it, but your decision will never be viewed as a mistake." That type of freedom will take BioPlus to greatness.

• • •

RHYTHM EXPERT TIP

Communicating and sharing the company's core values and purpose can help your team make the right decisions when you are not around. Make a conscious effort to thank team members publicly when their behavior demonstrates your core values or purpose.

Get your first two-day Think Rhythm session on the calendar. In the rest of part 1, I'll show you how to turn your Think Rhythm into a growth-generation habit.

Bottom Line

If you want to grow your company and focus your teams, you need a Think Rhythm.

→ Meet annually, quarterly, and weekly to work on the foundation of your company and develop winning moves to grow your business.

→ Put think time into your flight path: Schedule your Think Rhythm sessions in advance or they will not happen.

→ You can defeat a competitor who has significantly more capital if you put yourself on a regular Think Rhythm and use your resources with purpose.

→ Use your Think Rhythm to spend time having the right discussions. Free your team to voice opinions and share analysis. Do not rush to make strategy decisions. Instead, focus on having the right discussions.

→ Spend time refining and communicating the core strategy of your business so that your teams can make the right execution decisions with purpose.

CHAPTER 2

WINNING MOVES TO 2X YOUR BUSINESS

When you see a good move, look for a better one.

—Emanuel Lasker, chess grandmaster and world chess champion for twenty-seven years

Clear winning moves are one of the most important things you can have when getting your teams focused and aligned. They do not come from eureka moments. They are developed over time when you dedicate yourself to a Think Rhythm. Developing winning moves should be one of the top priorities of your Think Rhythm.

What are winning moves? Winning moves drive revenue growth. Specifically, winning moves should double your revenue—2X your business—in three to five years.

Why 2X? It's about your growth rate. Doubling your company in five years means that you are growing at about 15 percent every year. A growth rate of 25 percent doubles your business in about three years. So 2X over three to five years means growing at a rate of between 15 and 25 percent, compounded annually. By the way, you never want your growth rate to be slower than the rate of growth of your industry. To grow slower than your industry means you are losing market

Winning moves . . . do not come from eureka moments. They are developed over time when you dedicate yourself to a Think Rhythm.

share to your competition, despite your growth. If you happen to be in a fast-growth industry, you might have to plan to grow faster than 25 percent.

If you do not think about how to grow, you will not grow! If you do not have winning moves, you will not grow. And if you do not discover and execute your winning moves, your competition will. Companies that grow beyond a certain point can fall into the trap of believing that because they've grown in the past, they will continue to grow in the future. If you believe that, you will be blindsided. You need a Think Rhythm to develop strategies and winning moves and to execute those moves that will double your revenue in three to five years.

What about increasing gross profit margin by reducing cost of goods sold? Yes, moves that help you do that are good. Do those, too! But they are not winning moves. Improving gross margin is often an outcome of stronger, faster, and better execution. Great execution supports your strategies and complements your winning moves. But you cannot cut costs to grow. Only a strong strategy will help you increase revenue. The quality of your execution determines how much revenue the winning move ultimately generates and how much of that revenue hits your bottom line.

A friend of mine had a circuit-board manufacturing company that was doing well until manufacturing got outsourced to China. Under the competitive pressure of low-cost manufacturing, he worked hard to reduce costs and get more efficient. Unfortunately his efforts were not strong enough to win against low labor costs in China, and his company went under. Upon reflection, he wished that he had spent his time focused on opportunities in the market and creating a winning move instead of focusing inward on cutting costs.

The only way to sustain growth and avoid hitting the growth wall is to have a continuous supply of winning moves. At any time, you should be working on one to three. You never want to run out. They are your company's leading indicator for future revenue growth and

You cannot cut costs to grow.

Only a strong strategy will

help you increase revenue.

financial health. Conversely, the lack of winning moves is the leading indicator that you will hit the growth wall in the not too distant future.

Next to growth, the second greatest benefit of winning moves is focus. Winning moves give you focus. The stronger, more exciting your winning moves, the easier it will be for your team to stay focused and to say no to other ideas. That's what focus means. Saying no to other ideas and distractions.

Great winning moves wait for no man or woman! Use your Think Rhythm to develop the supply of winning moves you need for a brilliant future. Let's discuss techniques for brainstorming and ranking your winning moves.

The Secret to Developing Winning Moves

After facilitating hundreds of sessions, I have noticed some common patterns that might help you to brainstorm and develop winning move ideas. Let me share three questions you can ask yourself to reveal these patterns.

RHYTHM EXPERT TIP

It is sometimes hard to think outside the box when we are stuck with the same old patterns from our own industry. Attend trade shows and read magazines outside your industry. You might find new ideas that will work in your industry that also differentiate you from your competition.

What is your competition not willing to do that your core customers need?

Your customers may have a need that is not fulfilled because you and your competitors have not been able to provide a solution yet. Often, these are difficult problems to solve. The easy problems have already been solved, leaving the difficult and challenging problems for current players in the market to tackle. For example, I used to rent DVDs from Blockbuster. I wanted to return the DVDs to a different location, but Blockbuster said no. I had to return the DVDs to the same store that I rented them from. Enter Redbox. Redbox allows you to rent your DVD from one location and return it to any Redbox location. Think about what your core customers really need, instead of why it is difficult to take care of their needs, or how some of their needs may conflict with your products or services. If you can figure out a solution to any of these tough problems, you could have a winning move in hand.

What do your customers hate but continue to put up with?

Customers will put up with imperfect practices and solutions from us until someone else comes along and serves them better. For example, customers who rent cars put up with the exorbitant price rental car companies charge to fill up the gas tank when the cars are returned without a full tank (about three times the current retail price of gas). That is bad profit, earned by taking advantage of the customer. Yet customers will put up with it until a rental company decides to charge customers the current retail price for gas. That could be a winning move that differentiates a rental car company. What are your customers putting up with that could be the foundation of your next winning move?

Do I have a diamond in my backyard?
An asset that can be used?

It is difficult to appreciate what you have. The grass just always seems greener on the other side of the fence. We tend to overlook opportunities that are sitting right in front of us. Ask yourself, what assets do I have that might be transformed into a winning move? You might just have a diamond buried in your own backyard. This is the pattern that helped AvidXchange develop AvidPay. They noticed that they had an asset in their growing AvidInvoice network. They then asked how they could monetize it in a way that would bring value to both the customers and their vendors.

• • •

The right questions will lead you to the right answers. The right consultant or coach can be very helpful here. Armed with patterns that come from hundreds or thousands of hours of practice, a great guide or coach can ask questions that draw the right answers out of you. The key is to commit and take complete ownership of any winning moves that you choose to use. There may come a day when tough choices have to be made. At that moment, if you did not fully commit to the winning move, you might not have the emotional fortitude to make the tough decision to continue. It might be easier to write off the whole project as "that dumb consultant's idea" when success might be just around the corner. It is hard to dig deep and stay the course when it's someone else's idea.

RHYTHM EXPERT TIP

....

During your next annual planning session, ask each member of your team to take ten minutes and brainstorm five to ten potential winning moves. Collect the ideas and eliminate redundancies. Then list the ideas on a whiteboard and ask everyone to vote for three ideas. Count up the votes and take the top five ideas. Now go through the process of rating and ranking these five ideas. If a couple of these ideas turn out to be low impact on revenue, throw them out and pick the next couple from the list.

The right questions will lead you to the right answers.

Questions like the three I shared can help you identify a host of potential winning moves. Once you have figured out a potential list of winning moves, the next step is to prioritize them. To do that, I recommend rating and ranking them.

If you would like to brainstorm with more patterns, pick up *Outthink the Competition* by Kaihan Krippendorff. The four quadrant chart that I use to prioritize and think through winning move ideas was adapted from Kaihan's Path vs. Ease chart for assessing strategies.

How to Prioritize Your Winning Moves

To identify the best candidates for your winning moves, you need an objective and simple way to sort through ideas. Anyone's assessment of an idea when it is first put out into the world is subjective. We need an objective framework to discuss subjective ideas, to keep our discussions and decisions from becoming emotional. We also need an objective framework to separate winning moves from all of the potential losing moves. Your best ideas are the ones that will give you the strongest revenue growth for the least investment of resources.

I use a simple framework with two questions:

→ What is the impact on your revenue growth over the next three to five years? Using figure 5, rate the potential impact of your winning moves from 1 to 10, based on how much revenue growth the winning move can bring your company in the next three to five years. If you're trying to double your revenue sooner, use three years as your estimating time frame. If you plan to take a little longer, use four or five years. The higher the rating, the more revenue impact we expect. So 1 is bad and 10 is good.

→ How easy is it for your team to execute this idea? By "easy" I mean can it be implemented with current resources? Will it require little additional capital? Is it synergistic with other projects? Using figure 5, rate it 1 to 10. The more difficult or expensive it is to develop and execute, the lower the rating. When discussing how easy it will be to do, ask questions like

- What resources do we have now that we could use to implement it?
- What resources would we have to invest in?
- Would we have to develop other capabilities (through technological innovation or breaking into a new market) before we could make progress on this move? What would those cost in terms of our resources?

EASY TO DO

How easy is it to do?	Rare or expensive new capabilities	Need to hire new resources	Current team, impacts other projects	Current team, no impact on projects	Moves other projects along as well	Moves other projects along as well and teaches new skills
Rating (1-10)	1, 2	3, 4, 5	6, 7	8	9	10

IMPACT ON REVENUE GROWTH

Impact (3-5 Years)	0–50%	50%–75%	75%–100%	100%–150%	150%–200%	> 200%
Rating (1-10)	1–5	6	7	8	9	10

Figure 5. Rating charts for your winning-move ideas

- Would doing this make it easier to complete other winning moves we're currently working on?

Start with the two charts I've developed, but feel free to customize the ratings to fit your own needs. The important thing is to have an objective way to process and discuss the impact of these ideas without getting overly defensive of our own ideas.

Once you've scored your potential moves, plot them on the four-quadrant winning moves chart in figure 6. Where a move falls will tell you much about it:

→ **Green:** Winning moves (high impact, easy to do). These may seem like no-brainers. It's about delivering high-revenue growth while consuming few resources. The only reason you would hesitate is if you had too many of these moves. If you do, you'll have to prioritize them rather than try to execute them all at the same time.

→ **Yellow:** Expensive winning moves (high impact, difficult, or expensive). Moves in this quadrant may be winning moves, but only if they provide differentiation and create distance between you and your competitors. They are moat-building moves if they create barriers to entry for your competitors. But you cannot afford many of them. They may be expensive, or they may require resources you don't have. You may need new capabilities or market access that you don't have (which means spending more resources). However, when these moves strengthen your competitive advantage, making it harder for other companies to gain market share or enter your market niche, they might just be worth the investment.

→ Red: Losing moves (low impact). I call these losing moves because they may be difficult and expensive or easy and cheap. Either way, they pull valuable resources without delivering

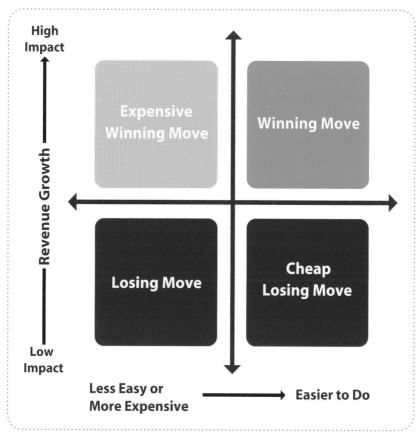

Figure 6. Four-quadrant winning-moves chart

good revenue growth. If they are relatively easy to execute, it does not make them any better. It only makes them cheaper! They still don't help us with strong revenue growth. And they might be distracting us from focusing on a few great winning moves. Companies do not choose low-impact moves on purpose. Often a great idea starts out as a high-impact move. Then, over time, we begin to realize that the impact is not as great as we had hoped or planned for. Instead of stopping our efforts, we continue without realizing the true opportunity cost. I'll talk more about losing moves in chapter 4.

Moat-Building Moves

Think of your share of the market as your castle. Most castles have a moat. When an enemy approaches, the drawbridge goes up and the moat protects the castle. The deeper and wider the moat, the better the protection. Now think of your current winning-move ideas. Which of your moves creates a barrier to entry for your competitors or a barrier to exit for your customers? These are your moat-building moves. They protect your castle, create differentiation, and give you more power to leverage against your competition.

Potential moves that fall in the top left quadrant of the winning-moves chart may be moat-building moves, or they may just be very expensive winning moves. If they are just very expensive winning moves, find a way to make them less expensive. Brainstorm ways to move them over to the top right quadrant. If you can't, move on. But if you have a move that truly differentiates you and is hard to replicate, building your competitive advantage, then consider if you can afford to invest in it. Expensive might be good, but only if it discourages your competition from copying you.

Apple's retail store concept is a good example of a moat-building move that worked. When Steve Jobs first announced that Apple was going to build stores, many experts *thought* it was a bad idea. When he unveiled the concept for the Apple store, breaking many of the rules of retail (for example, low product placement per square foot), the experts *knew* it was a bad idea. However, the Apple stores have been wonderful for Apple, giving them a competitive advantage. Even their well-heeled competitors have found it daunting to replicate this winning move. Apple clearly has their Apple store concept in a Think Rhythm. They did not stop at executing the Apple store, celebrating, and moving on to other things. Instead, over the last twelve years, they have continued to make their stores better. They added Genius Bars, reduced the cash-register space, and then removed cash registers totally. They now check you out on a mobile device. They also allow you to check yourself out using the Apple store app on your iPhone. Today, they have the highest sales per square foot of any retailer, more than double that of the second strongest retailer—Tiffany's! This success came about because Apple continued their Think Rhythm and still continue to improve their Apple store concept.

Be careful with moat-building moves. They take up a lot of time and resources. Most of us don't have unlimited resources that allow us to take on too many winning moves, especially expensive ones. The good thing about these moves is that they force you to become very focused. This is of course a double-edged sword, and overambitious leaders who lack discipline can end up killing a company by working on too many moat-building moves at the same time.

Use an Idea Bench

What should you do if you have too many winning moves? After you have rated and ranked your winning moves, choose the two or three that you want to execute sooner rather than later. Prioritize those that offer the greatest positive impact on revenue that take up the least resources to implement. In chapter 4, I'll offer a method for choosing a few from a lot of winning moves, a problem most of us wish to have. For now, know that you can put good ideas that are not prioritized on your idea bench. You are not saying no to these ideas. Rather, you are saying, "Maybe later . . ."

Create an idea bench and capture ideas from your think time that you aren't implementing now. Record outcomes of your discussions, especially the ratings you gave it and why. Don't lose all the expensive resources you spent talking about the idea. And don't make the originator of the idea feel like it was a waste of time to bring it up in the first place.

Bottom Line

Winning moves that ensure your growth year after year are not born overnight. Use your Think Rhythm to help you develop ideas and assess them.

→ Winning moves double your revenue—2X your business—efficiently, making the best use of your current resources.

→ To develop ideas for winning moves, spend time during your Think Rhythm asking questions that help you uncover opportunities. Don't be afraid to bring in an outside facilitator or a coach to help.

→ Test your ideas for revenue impact and how easy they would be to execute based on the resources required. This is an objective way for your team to discuss subjective ideas.

→ Don't be afraid to consider yellow moves (high-impact ideas that also take a lot of resources). But choose them only if they are moat-building moves that can give you a strong competitive advantage.

→ Choose two or three ideas to move forward based on potential revenue impact and how easy it is to accomplish. Put other good ideas on the idea bench for later consideration.

CHAPTER 3

5 STEPS TO DEVELOPING YOUR WINNING MOVES

Opportunity is missed by most people because it is dressed in overalls and looks like work.

—Thomas Edison

"Patrick began working with us at a time when we were completely stuck on how or when we might sell directly to consumers on our website." K.C. Walsh was reflecting on the time just before they had a strategic shift at Simms Fishing Products. Simms is the top choice of serious fly fishermen, especially professional guides, for high-quality apparel and gear. They make top-notch waterproof waders, boots, and fishing apparel of all types, designed to keep anglers warm and comfortable in the harshest conditions.

In my very first annual Rhythm session with them, they shared their thoughts on the future of the company: One winning move they knew they needed to pursue was to sell directly online, but they were hesitating. I asked them, "What has driven and continues to drive your success?" The answer was simple: People who are really passionate about fly fishing—professional guides and people who run specialty fly-fishing shops. *Hmmm.* I asked more questions. About two hours into the discussion it became clear that K.C. and his team were hesitating because they were worried that selling online could hurt their growth if they were not careful. Selling online could be a threat to specialty fly-fishing shops. These shops had grown significantly with Simms and were relying on Simms to continue growing in the future.

K.C. explains it well: "Our business not only had been built with these shops, but Simms and our industry is entirely dependent on keeping them healthy. This is a sport that requires hands-on assistance and expertise—people teaching other people how to fish, sharing a knowledge base of how to be successful. It's easy to see in this era that specialty stores are challenged by the web, and if you fast-forward five years, it's hard not to be concerned about their viability, particularly for those in states with high sales taxes. I just fundamentally feel that we cannot let that happen in our business. Without specialty fly shops, our industry really doesn't have a future."

They still had a problem, though. They were getting ten to twenty calls a day from frustrated customers who couldn't find the Simms products that they wanted, and were pretty annoyed that they couldn't buy them directly from the company. Solving that problem would be a winning move, but only if they could accomplish it without negatively impacting their retail partners.

Industry and strategy consultants had told them that by selling directly online, Simms would take some heat for about six months but then everybody would move on. Other manufacturers had taken the same approach. It would cause some friction between the company and retail stores, but retail stores had gotten used to this conflict as the new normal. But the leaders of Simms were just not comfortable with this idea.

If Simms could find a win-win way to help their specialty shops become even more successful as Simms sold online, it would make them quite different from their competitors. It might also encourage the specialty stores to provide them with more display space as compared to their competitors. I asked them a number of questions to explore this line of thinking: If you owned these stores, how would you include them in your online strategy? Building and owning stores is very expensive; is there a way to leverage these specialty shops as though you owned them? How can your online strategy also increase foot traffic to the local shop?

I shared a pattern that I had seen at REI. When something is not available at an REI store, customers can order online in the store and have the option of paying to have the item shipped to their home or having the item shipped to the store at no additional charge. They then come back to the store to pick up their orders, generating more foot traffic for the store. I noticed that I often chose the free shipping-to-store option—and ended up buying something else when I went in to pick up the order. Other retailers, such as Walmart, are now following a similar model. "What if you could do something similar?" I asked.

"But REI *owns* all their stores," K.C. said.

"Exactly! What if you could act in a similar way and have the specialty shops benefit from more foot traffic?" I asked. "Wouldn't they love you more and prefer to carry more of your products as compared to competitors who cause friction with online sales?"

The next step toward executing this winning move was to meet with a group of specialty online retailers who were selling Simms's products already. Together, they developed a system that would link people from Simms's site directly to product pages on these other dealers' sites when the customer clicked on a "Buy Now" button.

They kept on working on the winning move. They gathered more information and considered how they would support local shops. They developed a plan to make sure they weren't undercutting specialty retailers on price. They adjusted their plans as they learned more from the data they collected, even after they rolled it out.

So now, when you click on a product on the Simms site, you're given three options. The first one is to buy locally. Put in your zip code and you'll find out what shops in your area carry the product you're looking for. The second option is to buy from an online specialty dealer. The *last* option is to buy from Simms directly. And guess what? If you do, you're probably *not* going to get free shipping and you *are* going pay state taxes.

They had a winning move: Sell directly online. But if they hadn't continued to work on that move, talk about it, gather information and data, and test their assumptions, they may not have grown at all. In fact, they are still working on it. In session after session they discuss what's working and what isn't. They focus on that winning move and make adjustments to ensure it is successful.

• • •

RHYTHM EXPERT TIP

Set a realistic time frame to validate specific assumptions. Don't throw away the winning-move idea if an assumption does not pan out. If your assumption does not seem to work based on customer feedback and market testing, adapt! Change the assumption, and validate your new assumption.

In this chapter, I'll give you a process for using your Think Rhythm to work on your winning moves. Because once you have chosen your winning moves, it is time to get to work.

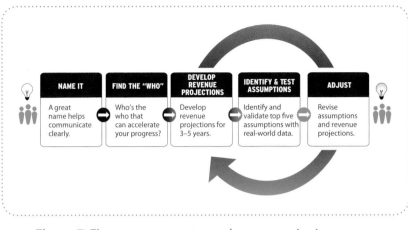

Figure 7. Five-step process to work on your winning moves

Step 1: Name Your Winning Move

Give your winning move a great name! Put some thinking into it. You will be using this name to communicate the idea. You will need to sell this idea both internally and externally. It's like naming a child. Put some thought into it and do it with purpose. Over time, as you work on your winning moves and learn more from real-world data and customer insights, your winning move might change or give birth to a new winning move. Name each winning move uniquely in order to communicate clearly with your team. It will improve your focus. Conversely, a poor name can be distracting and cause you to lose precious focus.

Step 2: Find the "Who"

Who can accelerate your progress? For example, AvidPay was a moat-building move for AvidXchange. It is incredibly hard to develop the necessary processes and security measures to get into the electronic-payment business. Many other CEOs Michael Prae-ger spoke to asked, "Why would you want to do that? It's so messy and risky." Michael and the AvidXchange team had to educate themselves on the electronic-payment business quickly. Many moat-building moves are like this. They force you into a new space where you don't have all the knowledge you need. In one of our Rhythm sessions, we discussed an important question: "Who's the who?" Who was the person (or people or group) who had great knowledge and experience in the area? Michael found a couple of people who could educate his team on the ins and outs of the payment process, and AvidPay moved forward quickly. The right "who" can significantly accelerate your progress!

Before you begin working on your winning move, set yourself up for success by gathering the best information from the most knowledgeable people. You might have to hire the right whos, either as a new team or as consultants. However you approach it, start by asking, "Who's the who who can help us?" You could potentially save months of time and substantial money.

Step 3: Develop Revenue Projections

Develop revenue projections for three to five years. Winning moves must bring you revenue growth. Answer the question, "What are our projections for the next three to five years?" As you move forward with the next steps, you have to circle back to your revenue projections. If data shows that they are off and the idea no longer helps you achieve 2X growth, the move is no longer a winning move and you might need to consider a stronger winning move in its place. This is the objective view of your strategies that you need in order to build the right focus for your organization.

Step 4: Identify and Test Assumptions

Your revenue projections are based on assumptions. Document these assumptions so that you can test and confirm with real-world data and customer insight.

Too often companies skip this step at the beginning and charge forward, wasting tons of resources only to realize at the end of the day that their primary assumptions were wrong. The idea results in significantly less revenue growth. If they had tested their assumptions, they could have made adjustments to make the winning move a success. In *Great by Choice*, Jim Collins suggests that you fire bullets before firing cannonballs. Fire bullets to test and verify your assumptions. You should have about five assumptions that you need to verify before you jump headlong into the winning move. Based on the real-world data you collect, if these assumptions do not play out to your expectations, your winning move might just be a losing move in disguise. Or it might just need an adjustment.

When I'm working with an executive team to clarify or discuss their assumptions, I often use the following questions:

→ Does this idea get us deeper with our core customers, or does it force us to service a separate and new set of customers? Would this be a good thing or a bad thing?

→ Does this make us more different or more similar to our competitors?

→ What gross margins do we think can be achieved?

→ What is the right business model? How does it contribute to our financial engine?

Remain open. Allow the right questions to lead you to the answers.

Most companies are used to the idea of tracking data for strategic initiatives and projects that have already been executed or are currently in play. A successful new habit to adopt is to gather data that you can use to test your assumptions before you unleash the full force of your company resources to implement this idea. Test your assumptions by firing bullets. Gather real-world data and insights. Recalibrate by making adjustments to your assumptions. And when you are finally ready, execute your plan violently!

To help you fire bullets, gather critical information, and work on your winning moves, using a Winning Moves Planner. I have included one here that you can download from the website. Use it to document your assumptions and collect real-world data. It should help you prove your winning move before implementing it, or it might help you decide to kill it before you get sucked into a losing move. Most leaders I know love their ideas. We do not typically come up with ideas and execute them with passion, all the while believing that they suck. No. We believe all of our ideas are winners. Unfortunately the world may not be ready for many of our ideas. The only way to know if your idea is a winning move is to track over time and discuss the moving pieces.

Your Winning Moves Planner should capture the following:

→ The winning move idea, desired result, and the scores for impact and how easy it will be to do

→ Revenue projections

→ Assumptions

→ Measurements: How will you measure and test each assumption? What does success look like? During each discussion, ask, "Are the assumptions we documented playing out better or worse than expected?"

→ Data: Gather whatever real-world data you can. From discussions with potential clients to testing a prototype, it is important to gather information that either confirms your assumptions or proves them wrong.

→ Insights: What insights emerge as you reflect on the data collected?

→ Adjustments: If you decide to make adjustments based on your discussions of the measurements, data, and insights, record them so that you know what adjustments you have made.

Use your Winning Moves Planner to take the drama out of discussing and executing winning moves.

Here is an example of how to use the Winning Moves Planner to document assumptions and test them. As you begin to test the assumptions, you will document your findings and insights in the green columns that are currently empty.

Rhythm™ Growth Tools			Winning Moves Planner		

Winning Move Idea

No.	Winning Move	Desired Results & Notes	Impact	Easy?
1				

5 Year Revenue Projections

Year					
Revenue					

Explore: Validate Your Assumptions with Real-World Data and Insights

No.	Assumption	How to Measure?	Real-World Data	Insights
1				

Rhythm™ Growth Tools	Winning Moves Planner

Winning Move Idea

No	Winning Move	Desired Results & Notes	Impact	Easy?
1	Product X	1. Revenues 2. Sticky (hard for customers to leave once installed)	9	2

5-Year Revenue Projections

Year	Year 1	Year 2	Year 3	Year 4	Year 5
Revenue	$1mm	$2mm	$5mm	$10mm	$25mm

Explore: Validate your Assumptions with Real-World Data and Insights

No	Assumption	How to Measure?	Real-World Data	Insights
1	Wallet share: > 50% of existing customers will buy this	% of customers buy		
2	Use existing sales reps	% of sales for each rep		
3	Market share: 50% of prospects who say no today will buy this product: opens new market for us	% of new customers who only buy X		
4	Validate government regulation R1 is in place for next five years	Jack to validate		
5	We will have at least one large channel partner to carry product X (Jill will approach five partners)	# Partners signed to sell		

Step 5: Adjust

Just because you've gathered information and tested your assumptions doesn't mean that your winning move has been perfected. You have to keep working on it. As you are working, you will make adjustments to the idea, you will revise your assumptions, and then you will test them to see if your assumptions are right and if your adjustments worked. Adjusting your assumptions will probably affect your revenue projections as well. So revise your revenue projections accordingly. This is the pattern of the Think Rhythm. Initially, you follow the pattern to verify that your idea is indeed a winning move. Then you follow it to keep your winning move from failing.

Repeat the adjust-and-test pattern until you reach a conclusion about the idea such as the following:

→ **Confirmed and ready:** You have the confidence to execute your winning move with extreme focus.

→ **Later:** You discover that while there is good revenue impact, the projections corrected by real-world data and insights are lower than other winning moves. Feel free to put this move on your idea bench for another time and replace it with a stronger winning move.

→ **Stop:** You discover that the assumptions did not pan out at all. This is really a losing move and not worthy of resources. Kill it and work on another winning move.

Once you decide to move forward with a winning move, keep using the pattern to make sure it remains a winning move. Successful winning moves take work. At each stage of execution, you need to adjust and test. Eventually, the winning move becomes an integral part of your company's operations and part of your Plan and Do Rhythms, so you can stop spending time on it during your Think Rhythm.

Bottom Line

Use your Think Rhythm to discuss your winning-move ideas and validate that they are truly winning moves.

→ Use an objective and systematic process to work on and validate your winning-move ideas.

→ Give each winning move a great name. Communicate and inspire your team.

→ Who's the who? Who can accelerate your learning and save you time and money?

→ Write down your revenue projections for each of the next three to five years.

→ Listen to Jim Collins: Fire bullets before you fire a cannonball. Identify your assumptions (bullets) and test them.

→ Use a Winning Moves Planner to take the drama and emotions out of the discussion process.

→ Recalibrate. Adjust your assumptions and test again. Repeat until you feel confident in your winning move. Then repeat until the winning move has been successfully executed and is a part of your weekly rhythm.

CHAPTER 4

YOUR "STOP DOING" LIST

Yesterday is not ours to recover,
but tomorrow is ours to win or lose.

—President Lyndon B. Johnson

At Metasys, we had a number of winning moves and products that drove us to hypergrowth. But we also had a couple of losing moves. In hindsight, I wish we had used a mechanism to force us to face the brutal facts—that the world was not ready for our products yet. (A nicer way to say that they sucked!) I wish we had shut them down long before we did. MetaXchange was one of those losing moves.

We were building interfaces between our flagship product, MetaFreight, and other enterprise software packages like SAP and Oracle Applications. Instead of programming custom interfaces for each customer, we decided to build a data-exchange tool that allowed us to map our interface tables to their interface tables. Great idea! It allowed us to scale our integration and speed up implementation for customers, significantly increasing revenue with our existing team.

Then we decided that if we could benefit from this, so could other software companies and internal IT departments of large companies. In fact, this was so cool, everybody would want it! Ever felt that way before? Oh, what a rush! Probably every time you birthed a new idea.

Nobody loses if a bad idea

is killed. Only the idea loses.

Everyone wins!

Anyway, it was a great idea until we decided to make it a product and sell it. Building something for internal use is a significantly different investment from building something for sale to the world. To sell it to the world, you need to have a complete product. That means you have to have better documentation, training, sales and marketing literature, salespeople, support people . . . the list of resources goes on! Anyway, we did all that and introduced MetaXchange—a supercool data-mapping product that we invested in heavily over the next three years—and earned revenue of $0. Yup: $0!

In the last chapter I talked about how helpful a Winning Moves Planner can be for tracking information that helps you test your assumptions. I wish we had had such a tool. We should have written down our assumptions and revenue projections and tested them. We needed an objective way to have our subjective discussions about MetaXchange. Was MetaXchange a product worth building? Was it worth the resources required to make it a sellable product? Who did we assume would buy it and did they? If we had recorded our assumptions along with real-world data, we could have killed that losing move much sooner. We could have saved millions of dollars of resources. But we got emotionally attached to the idea and we did not let it go when we should have.

It is normal to become emotionally attached to an idea after you work on it for a while. The more we invest, the more we believe that the idea is sound. But nobody loses if a bad idea is killed. Only the idea loses. Everyone wins! You save the company tons in resources and emotional energy, which you can apply to a winning move.

Two things happen when we become too attached to our ideas and winning moves. First, we end up working on losing moves, as we did at Metasys. Second, we try to work on too many winning moves and cannot execute any of them well. But a strong Think Rhythm can help us avoid these traps—traps that might have a hold on you right now.

Change is hard. People tend to wait until the pain of not changing is more painful than the pain of changing.

Stop Losing Moves

"I really dislike my business," a CEO I'll call Jack told me in one of our first meetings. "I can't seem to find a competitive advantage, and my net profit is between three and five percent. We're putting in a lot of hard work for very little return. I never really own my customers' business. As soon as a competitor comes in the door with a lower price, I have to negotiate like mad to stay in, reducing my margins even more."

I listened patiently to Jack's complaints. When he was through, I asked him to explore ways to increase his price using the same strategy frameworks that have helped thousands of companies. He needed to find winning moves to replace the losing moves—low-revenue-impact moves—that were killing his company. Jack shot down idea after idea. Unfortunately, this response is not that unusual. It is really hard to be open to new ideas. I have heard many of the same excuses from other entrepreneurs for why they continue to work on losing moves:

→ **"It pays the bills."** Really? Is that all you want to do? Pay bills? Why not take less risk and work for someone else instead of running your own business if all you want to do is pay the bills.

→ **"It's better than losing money."** Yeah, it is. But it is a lot worse than making great money!

→ **"I don't have a better alternative."** And you won't if you continue to let this move suck your time and energy away from creating winning moves.

Change is hard. People tend to wait until the pain of not changing is more painful than the pain of changing. But all they did was delay the inevitable. If you are hearing that same sucking sound that Jack heard, wake up! It is the sound of you slowly losing your life to a bad business. There are no good reasons to work hard on losing moves. Your life does not improve. Your company does not improve. And all the while, your competition is pulling further away from you!

Losing moves suck the life-force out of you and your company.

Expensive losing moves tend to be easier to identify and easier to stop because of the pain of wasting resources on them. Cheap losing moves—low-impact ideas that consume fewer resources—are harder to stop. Why? Because there is not enough pain. These losing moves take some resources, but not a lot. Like fool's gold, they appear worthy enough to continue wasting your resources on them in the hopes that they might pan out. But it's an illusion: Cheap losing moves suck just enough resources and focus to keep you from working on exciting winning moves.

Losing moves suck the life-force out of you and your company. They sap energy and morale. Your team is not stupid. They can tell when they are not working on anything game changing or important to the future of the company. You cannot encourage your team by working on losing moves. The famous phrase "The beatings will continue until morale improves" comes to mind. The only way to get your crew excited about the business is to get them excited about the future with true winning moves. Working hard for little return will slowly kill your company. Don't get sucked into working on losing moves.

But, you might be asking, how can I be sure I am working on losing moves?

How to Tell You're Working on Losing Moves—and How to Stop

Like winning moves, losing moves also do not happen overnight. Usually losing moves start out as winning moves. We get excited about the idea and jump into executing it before we have done a thorough discovery process, testing and validating the assumptions and business model, as suggested in the last chapter. Instead of firing bullets, we fire a cannonball. And once we start, it gets hard to stop investing in the strategic move, even if the revenue opportunity turns out to be significantly less than what we had expected.

Put your losing moves on your "Stop Doing" list to make room for new winning moves.

Here are five signs that you are trapped by losing moves:

1. Revenue growth has fallen to less than 50 percent of growth projections.

2. Customers are lukewarm about your new initiatives.

3. There is a lack of excitement and passion in your team when you discuss current strategy and initiatives.

4. Other ideas seem more exciting. You wish you had the time to take on more opportunities.

5. You are following the competition. When we do not believe in our own ideas, we tend to look toward our competitors and copy them. We become followers instead of leaders.

If you are stuck working on losing moves, it is time to de-suck yourself. Here's how:

Step 1: Stop. Decide to stop. Nothing changes if nothing changes. You have to choose to stop investing your time, energy, and resources on losing moves. It can be done. But you have to believe that there are

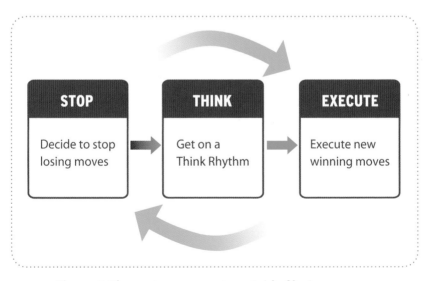

Figure 8. Three-step process to get rid of losing moves

great winning moves waiting for you. You can do this. The first step is the hardest. Take a deep breath and choose to stop working on your losing moves.

Step 2: Think. Get on a Think Rhythm. Begin thinking your way out of the problem. Use the Think Rhythm, but do not wait for the next annual meeting! Start immediately by spending half a day away from your office to think, on your own or with your team. Just do it. Empty your mind of the cares and crises of the company. Breathe. Do some yoga if you need to. Think instead of do. Work on your assumptions about current moves and your company in general. And don't get trapped by a losing move again.

Step 3: Execute. Execute your new winning move! Get rid of the drama and emotions.

It takes a lot of courage to stop losing moves, especially the cheap losing moves. Don't be afraid that you won't be able to replace them with real winning moves. You've done it before, and you will do it again. It is hard to quantify the opportunity cost of staying with losing moves but it is huge. You need to put your losing moves on your "Stop Doing" list to make room for new winning moves.

Stop Overeating from the Buffet of Opportunities

In an annual strategy meeting, CEO "Jill" shared her team's long list of great strategies with me. I asked them which one was number one. "All of them," they said.

"No, no, no," I said.

"Okay," one of the executives said, "1a, 1b, 1c . . ."

This company was very fortunate because they had many winning moves. However, not committing to a couple of strong winning moves to drive growth can cause death by overeating from the buffet of opportunities.

The best companies in the world focus on a few great ideas and say no to other good ideas. If you say yes to every good idea, your resources will be spread out over too many initiatives. Both the late Steve Jobs and Tim Cook of Apple have said, "At Apple, we say no to a lot of good ideas. These good ideas were just not as good as the ideas we said yes to." This focus has allowed Apple to rise to the top of the heap. Easier said than done, right?

Want to know if you've said yes too often? Check your project graveyard. Every company has one. It is where all the retired, incomplete projects rest in peace. Every tombstone in that graveyard represents wasted resources that could have been used to accelerate a few winning moves to market. Some tombstones are from the winning moves that you explored and discovered with real-world data and customer insight that they were indeed not winning moves. Those are the only good tombstones. They represent your commitment to innovation and discovering winning moves. All the other tombstones represent times when you were trying to do too much with too little. The result was a lack of focus and dedication to your best winning moves. In the end, very little got done, and the project died.

So let's talk about how to make no your new yes.

Won't Power

My wife and I were discussing the various things we wanted to do to maintain our diet and win the battle of the bulge. "We just need willpower to stop eating this junk!" I concluded. My eight-year-old daughter, Nicole, laughed. "Daddy, why do you keep saying that you need willpower? Isn't it actually 'won't power'? So that you *won't* eat those things?" After we laughed, we realized she was right.

Not committing to a couple

of strong winning moves to

drive growth can cause death by

overeating from the buffet

of opportunities. . . .

Make no your new yes.

Why is it so hard to say no to the pretty butterflies that fly by to distract you on your way to executing your strategic vision? The most common excuses that I've come across are

→ That looked like a really, really good idea at the time.

→ How could we say no to such a great opportunity?

→ We have a make-it-happen attitude.

→ We are entrepreneurs! Of course we must say yes to opportunities.

But if we resist, the benefits are incredible. Increased focus and energy for your chosen few winning moves accelerate your strategies to market. By focusing only on a few things, your team has the clarity to make the right decisions when different priorities and projects clamor for limited resources. Trade-offs are less difficult. Fewer projects that start, stop, or wait results in fewer tombstones in your project graveyard. With fewer priorities, you get stronger accountability for the success of the projects that matter most. And last but not least, things get done faster!

You don't need my help saying no to bad ideas. We all know how to do that. It is saying no to the good ideas that is difficult. Colin Campbell, the CEO whom I introduced you to early in the book, led Hostopia to strong continuous growth by focusing on a few winning moves. But it was a challenge. "Saying no to products and services—saying no to money—wasn't something we were used to," he said. They had a few key criteria to decide which winning moves they would focus on. One of their key criteria for a winning move was scalability. Another was their BHAG (Big Hairy Audacious Goal). Their BHAG was to win five million SMB clients paying ten dollars a month. Scalability had to be part of the equation to achieve their BHAG.

Their Think Rhythm helped them work through many questions on a regular basis. Which opportunities were the most scalable? Which opportunities would help them achieve their BHAG faster?

Which opportunities would help them focus on their core customers (SMBs) instead of causing them to take on customers that might take more resources to service? They were initially selling website-hosting services directly to consumers as well as wholesale, through telecoms like Bell Canada, EarthLink, and others.

"By analyzing what we knew and spending time discussing the opportunities, we learned pretty quickly that wholesale was our biggest opportunity for growth," Colin explained. "So we redirected our resources. We cut retail out. We learned that we had to say no to a number of opportunities and yes to the right ones." Saying no to retail was hard, but focusing their resources on wholesalers helped them become the leader in web hosting in North America, then Europe, then South America. Today, they provide services to many of the major telecoms on five continents and they have built technology partnerships with companies like Microsoft, VeriSign, and HP. They are on track to hit their BHAG.

Hostopia's framework for saying no is transferable. If you have a lot of potential winning moves, ask yourself

→ How does this help us achieve our BHAG? Does it help us get there faster than other possible moves?

→ Is this idea more scalable than others? Scalability leads to faster growth.

→ Will this help us service our core customers better than other ideas?

If you have more than a few winning moves (and be honest!) spend time during your Think Rhythm sessions asking these questions about each of them. Develop the won't power to put some of them on the idea bench and kill some of them outright. Use your Think Rhythm to grow faster, smarter, and with greater purpose today.

Bottom Line

If your growth is becoming stagnant or if you have a project graveyard with lots of tombstones, you need to use the Think Rhythm to find clarity and focus on a few winning moves.

→ De-suck yourself. Losing moves trap you. They suck your precious energy and resources and prevent you from developing winning moves.

→ Kill cheap losing moves. It can be hard to stop cheap losing moves. They do not eat up too many resources, so you let them linger. You are dying slowly from a thousand cuts while your competition zooms ahead!

→ Nothing changes if nothing changes. Stop your losing moves, develop a Think Rhythm, and put your time and energy into creating winning moves to 2X your company.

→ Commit to a few winning moves. Having too many winning moves can be just as detrimental as having losing moves. You know you have too many moves if you have a big project graveyard.

→ Develop won't power. Don't get distracted by new shiny ideas and opportunities. Stay focused on your winning moves.

→ No excuses! To find focus, you have to recognize the excuses you are using to keep doing too much and recognize the benefits of saying no instead of yes.

→ Stop. Think. Execute. Use this process to leave your losing moves behind!

THINK RHYTHM: 9 ACTIONS TO GET YOU STARTED

1. Get your free baseline assessment. Go to www.PatrickThean .com and take the free Rhythm Assessment before you begin this process.

2. Download the Winning Moves Planner to help you validate your winning moves.

3. Put think time into your flight path. Put your quarterly and annual sessions on your calendar now and communicate the schedule to the rest of the team. Make these meetings inviolate.

4. Work on your One Page Strategic Plan. Document your strategic foundations—your vision, your BHAG, your values, etc.—if you have not already. Spend upcoming think time discussing them with the team. Are they still valid? Do they create the right foundation for the growth you want?

5. Take inventory of your winning moves. Make a list of your current strategic moves. How many do you have? If you have more than five, you are spreading your resources too thin.

6. Assess your winning move ideas. Use the Winning Moves Planner to assess each of your current moves. Do you already have high-impact winning moves? Or do you have losing moves? Kill any losing moves now. Don't wait one more day.

7. Plan to win. If you discover that you do not have enough (or any) winning moves, put this on the agenda for your next quarterly planning session. Consider bringing in an outside coach to help facilitate the meeting. Have every member of your team read part 1 of this book to prepare for the session.

8. Use your idea bench. If you have more than five winning moves, you need to prioritize. Use the tools in part 1 as well as your strategy elements to prioritize the top five winning-move ideas and put the rest on your idea bench for later.

9. Fire bullets before cannonballs. Use the Winning Moves Planner to test and validate your assumptions before diving headlong into executing a winning move.

Part 2

PLAN RHYTHM

CHAPTER 5

GET YOUR TEAM FOCUSED AND ALIGNED WITH A GREAT PLAN

> One who is prepared and waits for
> the unprepared will be victorious.

**—Sun Tzu, *The Art of War*
(translated by Chen Song)**

Ever feel like firing everybody who works for you?

Ray, my partner at Metasys, walked into my office one day all flustered. I could tell he was having a bad day. You know the ones—the days when you can't believe you've gotten where you are and are still dealing with the same old stuff.

"Patrick! We have sixty programmers in R&D and we're turning out bad code! This is ridiculous! Some of it is bugs, but some of it is just bad judgment. With all of these mistakes, I feel like we're no better off than we were when you and I were writing code. We should shoot them all and you and I should cut code again." We had more people and resources, but it was harder to get things done right and we were getting frustrated. Everyone was running fast and working hard, yet our progress was slowing down because of rework and mistakes.

Yep. That's what a bad day feels like in a high-growth, successful

Lack of focus on a few things causes feverish execution that does not necessarily result in productive work.

company. Ever had one like it? Well, we did not fire everyone. Instead, Ray had a drink, calmed down, and went back to building great software.

In hindsight, I can see that we were not slowing down to plan our execution, so our team was not focused on the right things. This caused the mistakes and rework that slowed us down and reduced our profitability.

This happens in companies all the time. Lack of focus on a few things causes feverish execution that does not necessarily result in productive work. You start executing like ducks—paddling furiously below the waterline, yet moving slowly above the waterline.

When bad stuff happens in an organization, the first inclination is usually to blame the people. After all, people are producing the work. And when the work isn't completed fast enough or at the right quality level, it seems natural to ask if the people and teams know what they're doing. It seems less intuitive to ask if the environment is helping the people succeed. Most people I know don't join companies to screw them up or to be C players. "Hey, mum, I just joined company X and I can't wait to disappoint my boss and coworkers." No, I don't think so. Instead, the environment, process, and situation usually cause the poor outcome, not the people themselves.

If this struggle is familiar, ask yourself these three questions:

→ Does your team know what the company is supposed to achieve?

→ If your team does know what the company is focused on, do they know their roles in making that happen every quarter?

→ Do they have clear success metrics so they can tell if they are on track or not?

At Metasys, our people only knew some of the answers. Hindsight is 20/20. It seems clear to me now that we suffered from three things:

Just because a company is growing fast and its people are passionate does not mean that those people will magically understand what they are supposed to do to keep the company on course.

a communication gap, poor alignment, and lack of leading indicators. Decisions were not communicated clearly to departments and team members, so team members did not know what the company was focused on. We had a clear strategic vision and winning moves, and those are important. But we didn't have a specific plan every quarter for how we would execute to move forward. Without a plan, our teams did not know how to work toward the same goals. Everyone was rowing as hard as they could, but they were not rowing in unison. And without leading indicators, we did not know if we were off track and needed to make adjustments. It is so easy to celebrate results that have already happened. And we did achieve great results. But if we'd had forward-looking metrics (leading indicators), we might have avoided a number of crises. We could have prevented fires instead of fighting them. I discovered later on that fire prevention is much more cost effective than firefighting!

Like other hypergrowth companies, we claimed we did not have the time to slow down, plan our execution well, and communicate those plans to all departments. We didn't think we needed to. But just because a company is growing fast and its people are passionate does not mean that those people will magically understand what they are supposed to do to keep the company on course. Growth does not inoculate you against misalignment.

In fact, the faster you grow, the more important it is to take the time to slow down and plan with your departments and teams. Growth companies need a Plan Rhythm even more than other companies. Growing companies outgrow systems. As you've grown, have you upgraded your sales system and finance system, both the software and the methods used to make them productive and efficient? The answer is probably yes. But have you also upgraded or implemented a system to plan and execute your company goals, cascading them down to every department and employee?

If you do not implement a regular Plan Rhythm, you will zip right

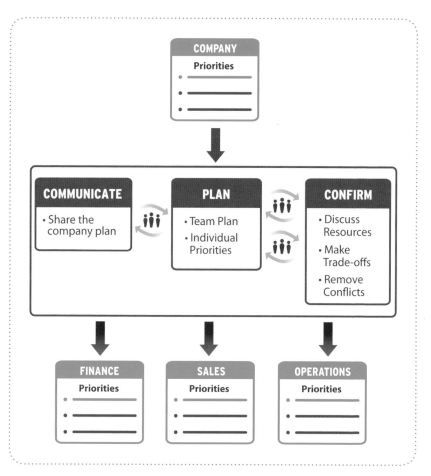

Figure 9. Cascade your plan to align every department.

by that exit without realizing it until it's too late. The results down the road will be rework and wasted energy, even when you accomplish the sales targets. You might not notice these execution mishaps, especially if you have strong revenue growth. People often achieve ambitious targets with superhuman effort. Strong revenue growth can cover most of your sins. But wouldn't it be better if our teams accomplished our ambitious targets with human effort instead? Because superhuman effort can only last so long. Without alignment, you will burn out your teams. You will either miss the opportunity to accomplish even more with your resources or miss your targets entirely.

Plan Rhythm: Execution Planning Is Different from Strategic Thinking

In a *Fortune* magazine article from 1999 entitled "Why CEOs Fail," Ram Charan wrote about famous CEOs who had failed not because they did not develop great strategies, but because they did not effectively execute those strategies. Effective execution requires an effective

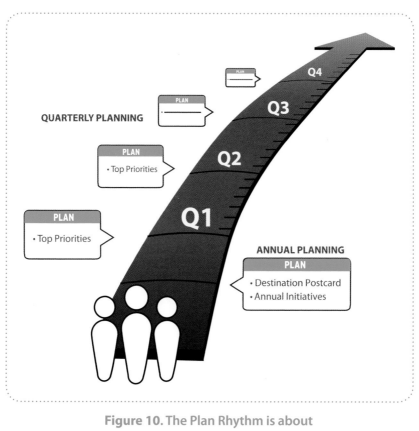

Figure 10. The Plan Rhythm is about figuring out how to get it done.

Setting up a Plan Rhythm is

relatively easy. Doing it well

is the hard part.

Plan Rhythm. Execution planning is not an event. You don't create a single execution plan once and for all. Instead, you create execution plans on a regular basis so you can adjust as you learn and gather insight from real-world experiences.

Many leaders confuse execution planning with the common term *strategic planning*. That is why I prefer to dissect the common practice of strategic planning into two separate and distinct parts: strategic thinking and execution planning. Strategic thinking is about figuring out *what you should do*. Execution planning is about figuring out *how to get it done*. It's your "doing plan." Oftentimes leaders focus only on strategy during planning sessions and forget to take the important step of working through an execution plan. It is easy to forget. After all, it is more fun to work on strategy. It's hard work to think about how to get the strategy accomplished. It is even harder work to hold your teams accountable for doing the work that achieves the strategy. This hard work *must* be done if you want your strategies to give birth to rewarding results. The teams that get into a regular Plan Rhythm execute. The process of planning together is part of the formula.

While the Think Rhythm is about choosing the right winning moves to drive revenue growth and focus your company, the Plan Rhythm is about preparation to align your teams and get them focused on the right things week by week and quarter by quarter. Great preparation gives the people in your company a much better chance to win when they take to the field against competitors. If you don't prepare for a great year, how can you expect to have a great year? If you don't plan for a great quarter, how can you expect to have a great quarter?

Setting up a Plan Rhythm is relatively easy. Doing it well is the hard part. Annual and quarterly planning are the key elements of the Plan Rhythm:

→ **Annual planning:** This is a two-day annual strategy and execution planning session. As discussed in part 1, the first day is spent on strategies for growth, as part of your Think Rhythm.

Spend your second day on execution planning. If your strategy is your "what," your execution plan is your "how." Do the hard work to figure out how to go about having a great year and how to make the vision exciting for your teams. Come up with the right few key initiatives to execute for the year.

→ Quarterly planning: This is a two-day quarterly execution-planning session. Spend the first day having discussions about how to continue executing your key initiatives for the year. Consider what has been achieved in the previous quarter. Discuss how your winning moves are coming along. Do they need any fine-tuning or adjustments? Use the second day to decide on the right priorities to execute. The right priorities should naturally emerge from the discussions you had on the first day. Your execution plan should consist of a handful of the right priorities that everyone is aligned around, specific metrics to track progress, and clear success criteria so that everyone knows what success looks like. A good execution plan will allow you to start every quarter with a clear picture of the desired results. This clarity empowers you to make adjustments to keep your annual plan on track. Cascading this process of execution planning to all your teams will help everyone get focused and aligned.

The Plan Rhythm is one of the most appreciated rhythms our team has implemented with successful leadership teams. They all rave about how it has changed their ability to grow because everybody is aligned to accomplish a few key priorities or initiatives each quarter and each year. Along the way, they have the visibility to adjust their plans when necessary to achieve their goals.

Slow Down to Go Much Faster

After a few planning sessions, Colin Campbell of Hostopia shared with me that the Plan Rhythm actually was saving time and resources. Having everyone in the room together allowed all angles on a topic to be discussed at once, leading to an execution plan that everyone agreed to and relied on. Having the right discussions up front instead of scheduling frequent meetings during the quarter accelerated projects. These discussions gave his leaders confidence and knowledge of other departments' priorities, which allowed them to plan with their teams. This process broke down silos and made every department more involved in solving problems, which led to more innovative solutions that took less time to execute. An unexpected benefit was that his leaders became stronger—better communicators, better collaborators, better thinkers and planners.

If you think you can't make time for these discussions, you had better find it. Because guess what? You are probably having these discussions anyway. Unfortunately, you are having them in the hallways or at the water cooler. You have part of a conversation with Jack, and then realize you should have pulled in Jill. You walk over to Jill's office and interrupt her to have this "urgent" discussion. Together you make a decision, but forget to update Jack. Now Jack's team and Jill's team start executing one degree out of alignment. This misalignment grows wider as execution progresses in both their teams.

A regular Plan Rhythm will make sure the right discussions happen with all key players present. It ends up saving you time, effort, and rework.

> ## RHYTHM EXPERT TIP
>
> The difficulty of scheduling planning sessions on everyone's calendar is the number-one reason these planning sessions are missed. Schedule your quarterly and annual planning dates a year in advance and publish them to a company-wide calendar. This keeps your executive team accountable to planning around those dates so they can attend, and it allows department leaders to establish their cascade-team Plan Rhythm for the year as well.

Close the Communication Gap

With growth comes complexity. With faster growth, the complexity is multiplied. Every project takes more time than you thought it would and you end up with a less-than-perfect result. Or, to your chagrin, you discover in week ten of a thirteen-week quarter that your team did not fully understand the vision for a project and now you have spent time, money, and resources implementing the wrong plan.

This is the *communication gap*. In the past, you were able to communicate plans rapidly. Your communication system was verbal and optimized for one-to-one communications. You were able to efficiently relay and discuss execution plans with the people on your team who actually did the work. Your decisions were also simpler. Opportunities to achieve your goals were fewer and the hurdles more evident. Now you seem to have an array of opportunities. You seem to have more opportunities than resources to deploy. Decisions are harder.

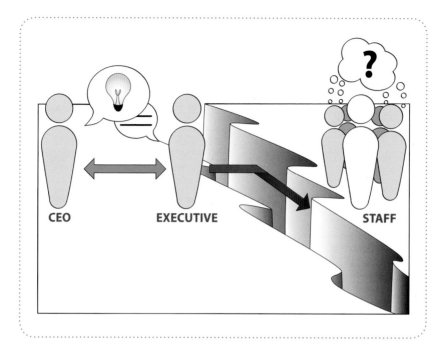

Figure 11. The communication gap: Does your team fully understand where the company is going and what they need to do? As companies get larger, this gets harder and harder to do.

The problem? You are now managing people who manage people who manage the people who actually get work done. You need a new way to communicate execution plans. You need a faster way to get information down to the front line and back up to the executive team so that everyone can execute with focus and alignment.

This is what the Plan Rhythm offers. It helps you close the communication gap that may be developing as you grow by giving you a regular rhythm for not only developing an execution vision and plan but also communicating that plan consistently to every person in your company. President Eisenhower once said that the act of planning is much more important than the actual plan itself. Planning with the executive team and cascading this process to your departments and

You are now managing people who manage people who manage the people who actually get the work done. . . . You need a faster way to get information down to the front line and back up to the executive team so that everyone can execute with focus and alignment.

all the way through the organization is a very effective way to communicate your story to your department leaders and then on down the line. Participating in planning discussions cements the goals and builds alignment.

A great plan should allow every person in your company to tell your story with clarity. Clarity in communication is critical to driving your execution plan forward with less waste and greater speed.

9 Tips to Running a Great Planning Session

When I first suggest to an executive team that they meet two days every year and two days every quarter to spend time thinking and planning, I see dread. Yes, dread. Most executives dread these types of meetings. They are usually boring and seem like a waste of time. How do you get them to be high-energy and productive?

These planning sessions are expensive. Maybe you've flown the members of your executive team in from around the country or around the world. You have pulled your highest-level leaders away from doing important work for two full days. These better be great planning sessions. Your executive team must leave excited, inspired, and totally ready to go out and kill the quarter! If you screw up, you have wasted your planning session. If you cannot pull off a darn good planning session, then hire a great coach or facilitator to help you. You have too much at stake to have a bad planning session. The value of these sessions better show up as increased revenue and profit.

Not all planning sessions are created equal. Here are nine tips to having great planning sessions.

Begin with the end in mind. Follow the advice of the late, great Stephen R. Covey. Be clear about the objectives of each planning session. Stay focused to achieve them.

Create a great agenda. Put lots of thought into the agenda. Let everyone know the agenda ahead of time. What are the few hot topics that you and your team need to wrestle to the ground together? Provide the agenda and discussion topics a week in advance so that your team can come prepared to work on those discussion topics and make good decisions.

Come prepared. Every executive needs to come prepared to participate fully in all the discussion topics. Spend some time before the session reflecting on the past year or quarter and gathering useful information or data. Think about what worked, what didn't, and what adjustments you would make knowing what you know now. Leaders should ask their teams or departments. Don't fall into the trap of thinking that you have better answers than your team members, who are closer to the work, or closer to customers. Have discussions with your teams ahead of time on the agenda topics. Get their data and insights.

Use a facilitator. It is an expensive day for your team. Invest in a facilitator to maximize productivity. It is very difficult to participate and facilitate, especially if you are the CEO. Ask yourself, "Do I want to facilitate, or do I prefer to participate and engage strongly in the discussions?" If participation is more important (and it usually is), bring in an outside facilitator. I have often found that CEOs who facilitate their own planning sessions unknowingly intimidate their team members and limit their participation in the discussion. The power of the CEO's position combined with the power of holding the facilitator's pen is just too overwhelming. It sets up an environment in which the team is more comfortable being told what the CEO wants them to do than contributing their ideas and opinions.

Set the right tone. Begin every session by having each team member share good news or appreciation. Beginning on a positive note will improve participation. It is also a good way to get people to warm up their vocal cords and get into the flow of talking and sharing ideas.

Be effective versus efficient. Spend the time necessary to have the right few discussions. Don't rush your planning session by focusing on getting through all the topics on your agenda. Instead, choose to be effective. It is better to have fewer discussions, with the entire team understanding clearly what the decision and outcome is for each. A great facilitator will slow the pace of the meeting in order to get to good decisions on sensitive or emotionally charged topics. If team members feel rushed and do not feel that their opinions have been heard, you will not be able to achieve alignment and agreement. An agenda is important, but do not get so stuck on the agenda that you cut off important discussions just to try to cover every point. Make time to discuss, debate, and agree, something I'll talk much more about in the next chapter on annual planning.

Use a parking lot. Tangents to the important topics are inevitable. Use a parking lot to log these tangents for a later discussion. It allows the team members who bring them up to know that they will not be forgotten. Then their brains are free to focus on the topic at hand.

Eat the baby elephants. Every company has elephants in the room. The fewer the better! These are the topics that the team tries to avoid because they are afraid to address them. Lots of emotional energy is wasted over the years skirting around these topics. Once upon a time these were baby elephants. If you see a baby elephant surface during your sessions, take the time to address it. Eat your baby elephants before they grow up into big seven-ton elephants!

Cut it off when the team is tired. You won't get good decisions when people are too tired to think. If you have had intense discussions, everybody will be exhausted toward the end of the day. End the meeting on a victory. Don't "power through" the agenda. Have a backup plan to spend some time the following day finishing up if necessary. And if you are making big decisions, think about them overnight and have a brief discussion the next day to finalize them.

RHYTHM EXPERT TIP

CEOs should spend more time listening than speaking at these planning meetings. You don't get many opportunities to listen to what your teams are thinking. Be curious and listen—actively—and be the last one to provide your input.

· · ·

The Plan Rhythm is your best chance for successful execution. What doesn't get planned usually doesn't get done. With the right approach, your sessions can be productive and inspiring and can create the alignment you need to grow. In the rest of part 2, I will help you learn how to implement a strong Plan Rhythm and make it successful.

Bottom Line

The Plan Rhythm is essential to great execution planning that builds alignment throughout the organization.

→ Meet annually and quarterly to plan your execution for the year and for the quarter.

→ Separate execution planning from strategic thinking. Execution planning is figuring out how you will get work done to move your company forward quarter after quarter, year after year.

→ Planning requires you to slow down, and the result is that you execute faster and with less waste. If you are not making the time to plan, you may be wasting resources on inefficient execution and ineffective communication.

→ Planning with your team closes the communication gap that comes from hiring more employees and managers to support growth. It provides a structured way to create a plan and communicate that plan throughout the company to build alignment.

→ Your teams must be totally inspired to have a great quarter! Here are nine tips to have darn good planning sessions: Begin with the end in mind, create a strong agenda, come prepared, use a facilitator, set the right tone, focus on being effective rather than efficient, use a parking lot, eat baby elephants, and cut it off when the team is tired.

CHAPTER 6

DEVELOP AN INSPIRING PLAN

*The future belongs to those who
believe in the beauty of their dreams.*

—**Eleanor Roosevelt**

The Berlin Olympics, 1936. The Germans were sweeping the crew events. They had won five gold medals and one silver medal leading up to the final eight-oar two-thousand-meter race. The Huskies were representing the United States. And they were not the typical winning crew team.

This team of nine (eight rowers and one coxswain) had beaten incredible odds to get to the Olympics that year. First, they weren't the typical Ivy Leaguers from Yale, Harvard, or Princeton. Second, their journey had begun just twelve months before, when they were first put in a boat together at the University of Washington. Third, they weren't even the first boat for the university when they were initially teamed up. How did they leap from second-tier at a university that had never beaten an Ivy League school to representing the United States at the Olympics? They developed an inspiring vision by focusing on where they wanted to be in a year. They referred to their vision as "LGB." While they let other people think it meant "Let's get better," the team knew it meant "Let's go to Berlin."

Aligned on this singular goal, the team quickly became the first boat. They thought hard about how to beat their competition and developed a winning move. They would maintain a stroke rate slower than the competing boats, allowing their opponents to build up a lead while they conserved their energy. Then at the right moment, their coxswain, Bob Moch, would call upon the team to bring their stroke up to an incredible rate of thirty-five strokes per minute. In perfect alignment, the team would put their boat, the *Husky Clipper*, into a sprint, come from behind, and win the race. They worked on their execution of this winning move week after week, month after month. It worked every single time. They broke records and won races that had never been won by a non–Ivy League team. And they earned their spot at the Olympics.

Even then, the journey to the Olympics was not easy. These young men went to a state university and all came from middle-class backgrounds. They worked their way through college doing janitorial work, selling tickets, ushering at the stadium. They didn't have the money to sponsor their trip to the Olympics, and the school did not either. But their passion for their vision did not waver. With a big local push for donations, they raised the necessary $5,000 and got third-class tickets on a ship to Berlin.

The day of the final race, they faced what seemed like insurmountable odds: an ill oarsman, poor lane position, wind and rough water, and seventy-five thousand screaming German fans. At eight-hundred meters from the finish line, they were far behind the other boats. Yet their inspired focus and alignment enabled them to execute their winning move with astounding power. Bob Moch began their sprint, bringing their rate up to an unheard of forty-four strokes per minute, a rate higher than they had ever rowed before. At five-hundred meters out, they had pulled into third place. And at three-hundred meters out, they had pulled even with Germany in second position. The announcers were going wild. The last one-hundred meters of the race were a blur for the Huskies, and when the Americans, the Germans, and the Italians crossed the finish line, the Huskies had won by 0.6 seconds! (USA 6:25.4, Italy 6:26.0, Germany 6:26.4. After almost six and a half minutes of racing, just one second separated the three boats.)

The Huskies did not simply get to Berlin—they won. They won because of a destination they envisioned that gave them purpose. That purpose aligned their efforts and inspired them to execute consistently and to the top of their abilities throughout the year. But their execution at the race was legendary, and I'll tell you more about how they won in part 3. The crew team is my favorite metaphor for great execution. You do need strength to win. But strength is table stakes. Every competitive crew team has strength and endurance. The winning crew teams must also have superb alignment and inspired focus.

Give your teams purpose by developing an inspiring annual plan.

Are You Building a Cathedral, or Just Laying Bricks?

You need an annual plan that will ignite the passion and imagination of your team. To do that, your plan cannot just be about hitting financial targets. It must inspire by connecting to your long-term goals and purpose. A good question to ask is "What will make this year special and memorable in the history of our company?" A great annual plan needs to describe how you will achieve goals and targets logically as well as inspire the hearts of the team. In other words, people in your company must connect with it both logically and emotionally. To ensure that happens, once you have developed your plan, you need to tell your story to the rest of the company in a clear and compelling way.

The second day of your annual planning session should be spent

A great annual plan needs to

describe how you will achieve goals

and targets logically as well as

inspire the hearts of the team.

developing your inspiring plan of attack for the year. You should finish the second day with an annual plan that includes

→ An exciting main focus for the year

→ No more than five key initiatives to help you achieve your main focus for the year

To grow, you must devote energy to your winning moves throughout the year. But you cannot focus all of your energy on only doing new and innovative things. That's not practical. You need to work on new initiatives and work on running your current business well. So a couple of your initiatives should be focused on growth and a couple should be focused on flawless execution of your current business.

That said, most companies neglect the inspiration component of their annual plans. So that is where we always start.

Lots of companies create an annual plan each year. But do those plans actually bring focus and alignment to their teams? Oftentimes when I ask CEOs what their year is about, they tell me their financial goals: "This year we are going to hit forty-five million in revenue with a twenty percent profit!" "We are going to grow by a hundred percent!"

I am reminded of the story of Sir Christopher Wren. Sir Christopher Wren was commissioned to rebuild St. Paul's Cathedral after the Great Fire of 1666 in London. One day in 1671, he observed three bricklayers working hard, yet with different quality. He asked them what they were doing. The first bricklayer replied, "I am working, laying bricks." The second said, "I am building a wall." The third, the one who was doing the best quality work of the three, said, "I am building a cathedral."

If you only think about your year in terms of financial goals, then I am sorry to say, you might just be laying bricks or building a wall. Instead, make it memorable in the history of the company, not just another year of numbers that you can hit or miss. Give your year a strong, exciting purpose.

If you only think about your year in terms of financial goals, then I am sorry to say, you might just be **laying bricks or building a wall.**

Dan and Chip Heath described the destination postcard in their book *Switch*. They defined it as a "vivid picture from the near-term future that shows what could be possible."[2] The point is that to grow and change, you have to know where you are headed and be inspired by what is possible in the near term. This is exactly what our successful clients have been doing year after year. It is part of their Plan Rhythm.

To help them create their destination postcards, we've developed the Time Machine Exercise. The Time Machine Exercise is designed to help you think outside of the box, to use your imagination to envision how great the year could be. The goal is to develop a narrative for the year that helps you consider not only what you will *do*, but also how the success of the year will make you *feel*. This is the critical emotional piece. If you cannot see it, you cannot make it happen. And if you cannot feel it, you cannot inspire others.

Use the Time Machine Exercise to help you begin with the end in mind.

Time Machine Exercise

To use the Time Machine Exercise in your planning session, start with independent work by each team member. Once you have each worked through the steps below, you can discuss your ideas and write yourselves a postcard from the future.

> → **Step 1: View the present from the future.** Step into your imaginary time machine and travel to the end of the year that you are planning for. Step out of your time machine and describe what you see from the vantage point of the end of the year. First, write a description of what the company achieved. Why was it such a great year? Such a memorable year? Since you are writing from the future, use past tense, as though the year

2   Chip Heath and Dan Heath, *Switch: How to Change Things When Change Is Hard* (New York: Crown Business, 2010), 76.

has already happened. Have some fun here. This should be an imaginative exercise. Second, identify the top three things or initiatives that made the great year possible.

→ **Step 2: Share your destination postcards.** Have each team member share his or her destination postcard. Observe carefully which phrases generate the most excitement from the team. There is a good chance that the company's destination and main focus for the year will be captured in more than one narrative. Then, as each person shares ideas for the three things that led the company to a great year, make a list of possible key initiatives. Put a check next to each idea every time another team member mentions it.

Michael, We pull this card out together and celebrate a very successful 2012 for AvidXchange
1. We ignited a revolution with Automated Bill Pay
2. AvidPay rocks with 40+ clients in multiple verticals
3. We developed a strong strategy to monetize float in 2013
4. We have 350+ clients at 97% retention & a strong sales engine
5. We added great people and our leadership program rocks!

And of course we exceeded our financial targets . . . Yeah!

You call me to celebrate "Patrick, thank you and your Rhythm Team for helping us achieve another great year..."

"Now, for 2013, we need to . . . "

Figure 12. Destination postcard for AvidXchange

Here is an example of a destination postcard that I sent to Michael at AvidXchange after his 2012 annual-planning session. The year 2012 was special for them. They were inspired to achieve their destination postcard. It was the year they launched their electronic bill-payment business (AvidPay).

If you are already sure of the main focus for the year, you can use this exercise to get everyone to focus and develop ideas for how to achieve that goal. You can also use this same exercise for any planning time frame. For instance, when you are building a three-year plan, you can frame the exercise to discover which winning moves will help you achieve the success you saw when you stepped out of your time machine.

Once you have a strong, inspiring vision for what the year will bring, it's time to dig in and develop the execution plan that will get you there.

How to Execute Your Strategy

The Time Machine Exercise is an effective visualization exercise. It should generate a lot of great ideas for your main focus and initiatives, but not all of the ideas that emerge may end up in your final plan. When refining your list of initiatives, you should choose the few ideas that have the greatest potential to move your strategy forward.

Say Yes to the Right Things and No to the Others

In 1991, when I left Oracle to start Metasys with a couple of buddies, I was a twenty-six-year-old software developer with a dream of building a software company—a big, bad public software company just like Oracle, aggressive in marketing and focused on performance. This was our BHAG. I just did not know to call it that back then! The only problem was that we were a custom consulting shop, not a software company. But we were guided by our vision. We were singularly focused on this objective. By 1996, we were a $5.2 million business and we decided that this was the year we would make a leap forward. We did something that few businesses would have the guts to do.

We abandoned $1.7 million of consulting business, and burned our boats along the way. We shut down our Oracle custom-consulting business entirely and focused all of our resources on being a supply-chain software company. A million and a half dollars and change isn't a lot of money if you're a big company, but it was 30 percent of our revenue. I needed every person in the company to help with our transition to a supply-chain software company. The decision was very painful but easy. At our spaghetti junction of opportunity, we allowed our BHAG to guide our decision. We believed that we would be much more successful and scalable as a supply-chain software company. We did not have the resources to be great at both. We were fully committed to our BHAG. And within two years Metasys was a supply-chain software company with over $20 million in revenue. That's what can happen when your team has single-minded focus.

Most of our clients have a similar story of growth. They do not lack in opportunities. Rather, they had to develop the courage to say yes or no to opportunities that came their way. If you feel torn, let your BHAG decide for you. Ask the following questions:

→ What obstacles are in our way that we must overcome this year?

→ Are there any immediate threats out there that we should address?

→ Are there any new opportunities that we should discuss now and possibly incorporate into our plan for the year?

→ Do these opportunities get us to our BHAG faster? Or are any of these opportunities detours?

Choose the one or two opportunities that take you closer and faster to your BHAG. Say no to the other opportunities that are potential detours.

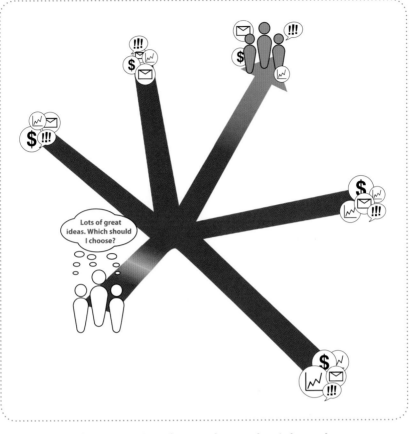

Figure 13. How do you choose the right path
at the spaghetti junction of opportunity?

Accelerate Your Winning Moves

For AvidXchange, 2011 was a very special year in the company's history. It was the year they built their AvidPay (electronic payment) product. They began with a plan to develop AvidPay in twelve months, meaning it would go live sometime in the middle of 2012. But as they discussed the move, they realized that AvidPay was not just *a* winning move. It was *the* winning move. Being the first to kick butt as the leader in online payments for midmarket businesses was critical. They wanted to launch this game-changing product faster and surprise their competition. That's when Michael Praeger and his leadership team made the decision. They had to get AvidPay done in six months and launch it at the beginning of 2012.

During one of their planning meetings, they crafted an execution plan that made AvidPay the main focus for the rest of the year. Michael asked, "Wouldn't it be cool if at the end of January, we cut our first electronic payment check?" This was their destination postcard and it gave them a single point of focus. This single point of focus allowed them to move other competing priorities aside and make this main focus a reality. Everybody wanted to get that first e-payment done and was focused on what they could do to make it happen. It was inspiring and exhilarating.

This main focus was communicated to every department and team. They built their priorities to support it. They found better ways to get there by making the right trade-offs and decisions. Usually, various stakeholders will push hard for their product agendas. But the inspiration of their destination postcard combined with the clarity of their main focus of delivering their first e-payment helped everyone make the right trade-offs. It was so compelling that it broke down their silos. Every department, every person in the company wanted to find ways to accelerate the development of AvidPay. It pulled everyone together to find solutions to keep current clients satisfied while a development team focused on the new product. All because everyone's head and heart was committed to delivering an e-payment by January 31, 2012.

AvidXchange *was* able to deliver their first e-payment on January 31, 2012. The launch of AvidPay generated $650,000 of revenue in 2012. More important, they went into 2013 with $3 million backlog committed, on their way to achieving their $5 million goal for Avid-Pay for 2013.

During your Think Rhythm session, review insights on your winning moves with the team. How is the implementation coming along? Are you on track to experience the growth that you expect from them? During your Plan Rhythm session, ask, "What are we going to do this year to realize the promise of growth from these winning moves?" Let this question guide you in building your annual plan. Say yes to your winning moves and no to other distracting opportunities.

RHYTHM EXPERT TIP

It's really hard to stay focused and say no when a new potential opportunity comes up and distracts you. The only way to do that is to have a future so compelling that you really don't want to pursue anything else. So if you find yourself attracted by other "pretty butterflies," you might need a more compelling future to stay focused.

Discuss, Debate, Agree

Even with the guidance of your vision and winning moves, you will still likely have lots of good ideas on the table. It can be hard to get the team to agree to a clear destination and focus on a few initiatives.

When it comes to priorities, less is more. At Rhythm Systems, we have thousands of executives setting priorities in our Rhythm system. The pattern we see over and over is that those executives who have five or fewer priorities achieve a strong result. But when an executive is

Executives who have five or fewer priorities achieve a strong result. But when an executive is loaded with seven or more priorities, only two get done well, and the other five or six are not completed.

loaded with seven or more priorities, only two get done well, and the other five or six are not completed.

This pattern shows us that there is a tipping point. When we cross that tipping point in the number of priorities on our plates, it is not just the extra one or two that don't get accomplished. Rather, we are rendered ineffective across the board because we lack focus. What is worse is that we are not even aware of which priorities will get done well and which will fall off the wagon. You are better off deciding what is truly important than having a long list and hoping that it will all get done through hard work. Choose your priorities or fate will choose for you.

To get your team truly aligned with the few right things, you have to help them release the pet projects in their heads and hearts and sign up for the few that are selected by the whole team. If you do not accomplish this in your planning sessions, your team will walk out seemingly aligned, but they will continue to work hard on pet projects. In fact, they might not even realize they are not aligned with the rest of the team until it shows up in their actions. I have found that this happens for two reasons: (1) The decision was made so fast because there were so many things to talk about that they did not get the chance to express their opinions about alternatives. People did not feel heard. (2) They did not fully understand the decision and were not given the time to discuss it enough to personally connect with it.

Having team members with different opinions is a good thing. If we all have the same opinions, most of us are just cost-saving opportunities! You can still achieve alignment even if you have different opinions. You just need to give team members the opportunity to express their opinions until they feel they have truly been heard. Once we feel heard and understand others' opinions well, we are willing to embrace an opinion that is not our own, and execute it. To do this, we need be able to discuss, debate, and come to agreement.

Having team members with different opinions is a good thing. If we all have the same opinions, most of us are just cost-saving opportunities!

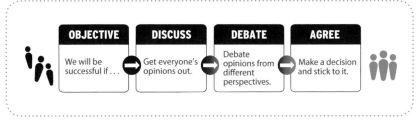

Figure 14. Discuss, debate, agree process

Try this process to help you discuss, debate, and agree:

→ **Step 1: Identify the objective.** State the objective clearly. Ask the team to complete the statement "We will be successful if . . ." If you do not begin the discussion with the end in mind and know what success looks like, you have already lost the opportunity to achieve agreement before you begin.

→ **Step 2: Discuss.** Get the opinions out. Write them down on a tear sheet or on the whiteboard in the room.

→ **Step 3: Debate.** Encourage debate. Here is where many discussions fail. It is normal to feel uncomfortable when team members have different opinions. Instead of stifling different opinions, your facilitator should encourage the airing of different opinions. What key discussions do you need to have so that you can be aligned for the year? Are there any issues that you cannot discuss and therefore need to? Eat the baby elephants.

→ **Step 4: Agree.** Decide on the solution or the outcome. It is important to note that agreement does not necessarily mean that everyone arrived at the same decision. Make it clear who the decision maker is on this topic, and after all opinions have been heard, allow the decision maker to make the final decision. Commit to the decision. Pause and ask everyone in the room to commit to the decision made. This is the "agree" part of the process. Here is where people release their own agendas and agree to execute the plan that the team created.

The result of the discuss, debate, agree process should be a team commitment to the decision made, with everyone moving forward aligned, just like a championship crew team.

Having the right process is key. Yet different facilitators armed with the same process can arrive at different results. Success is in the nuances of how facilitators help you through the difficult discussions. Here are some tips for facilitators:

Your facilitator should allow breathing space during discussions. Do not feel compelled to fill periods of silence. Let the silence do the heavy lifting for you. These are the best moments. Allow the team to consider what others are saying. Brief periods of silence encourage deeper thinking and discussion on the topic. At the opposite end of the spectrum, when the debate gets too hot, the facilitator should remind everyone that there are no losers when we discuss and debate. Only the less-good ideas lose. And when that happens, we are all winners.

The facilitator should also encourage the silent ones to speak up. Make sure that everyone has had the opportunity to share their opinions and participate, especially the people who are typically quiet. Encourage them to speak up. If you are the CEO, you can help. You probably do not often get the chance to bring your entire team together for this type of focused work. Take the opportunity to listen to their ideas and input versus telling them what you want done. Spend the time listening instead of talking, and offer your opinion on any topic *last*.

Most important, the facilitator should guide the team to a decision. I have seen teams spend an hour in a heated debate only to end without a decision. Making a decision is difficult. Remind the decision maker that it is his or her decision to make. Ask if there are any more points to debate. And if not, gently let the decision maker know that it might be time to make a decision soon.

Create a "won't do" list. Finally, as the team reaches agreement on initiatives for the annual plan, you might need to create a "won't do" list. Recall that I described the importance of won't power in part 1. If you have too many opportunities, take the time during your annual planning session to discuss, debate, and agree on the "no" decisions. When you make a no decision, record it. You'll be recording your yes decisions as part of your annual plan. Record your no decisions and your reasoning so that if you are tempted by those same opportunities during the year, you can remind your team why you said no to them in the first place.

Gaining agreement and closure on key topics is critical to closing the communication gap. If you cannot agree at the executive-team level on the few important elements of your annual plan, you cannot hope to cascade plans and decisions to the departments and other teams. That is what closes the communication gap and builds alignment.

Avoid Common Pitfalls

At Rhythm Systems, our coaching team has had the opportunity to work with clients around the world. These are the most common pitfalls we have noticed in the annual planning process.

Vague Plans

Your plan must have execution details and specific milestones. Inspiration is not a good excuse for not being specific. You must have both. You must also have details and specifics to hold the team's execution accountable to the plan. I have seen companies create inspiring plans that are either too vague to be applied to the work of teams or too ambitious to be realistic. A few months into the year, the plan is abandoned and by the end of the year, nothing strategic has happened. The year was almost meaningless in the history of the company.

To avoid this pitfall, create a plan with specific milestones. Test your initiatives and set yourself up for productive quarterly planning. We recommend creating a four-quarter flyover plan. It's easier to edit than to create. With a flyover plan, you won't have to start from scratch each quarter.

What will you do each quarter to make sure that each of the initiatives is executed and that you reach your destination at the end of the year? Do not get into specific details of how you will execute each quarter. Things will change as the year progresses, and you will have to adjust. What you thought you might accomplish in the second quarter has to wait until the third. Or an execution stage took less time than you expected and you need to adjust the plan for the rest of the year. That is why you plan the details of execution each quarter. For the flyover plan, just think about big-picture quarterly progress.

Once you've created a rough plan for the year, look at what you have noted for each quarter. Are you managing your energy appropriately? Is it realistic to think that you will accomplish what you have outlined? If not, reassess your annual plan and refine your initiatives.

Lack of Communication

A plan is also useless unless everybody knows about it and supports it. Share your plan with everyone so that you can close the communication gap.

After the executive team creates the annual plan for the company, they should share the plan with all department leaders. Each department should then develop an annual plan that supports the company's plan. The process for creating those department plans is usually similar to the process I've described already, but it should take less time.

The big-picture plan has already been created. The department plans should manage team members' energy to ensure that the daily work of the core business is accomplished and that the growth initiatives or winning moves of the company's plan are supported.

Once the department plans are completed, have an annual kickoff meeting for all employees. You might do this all together, you might do a teleconference, you might do it in separate groups around the globe. However you do it, make sure you are ready to help every employee understand and connect with the plan. First, use the work you did on your destination postcard to talk about what achieving the main focus for the year will mean to the future of the company. Get people excited about the opportunities the planned growth will create. Inspire them!

After you inspire them, ask every team member to consider two questions:

→ What does this plan mean to me?

→ What can I personally do to help?

These are questions that will help them connect with the plan logically and think about how to support the plan in their daily work. Without that level of support all the way through the company, a plan cannot succeed.

Acceptance of Mediocrity

You get what you accept. If you accept mediocrity, you will receive mediocrity. What if you were not able to build a compelling plan for the year? Do you compromise and accept mediocrity? No! If you do, you will waste the year. Sun Tzu writes in *The Art of War* that you should only go into a battle when you are certain of victory. If you are not satisfied with your execution plan for the year, spend the time and energy needed to fix it. Go into the year certain of victory. Think about it. You are about to commit all the resources and lives of your company to a new year. If you can't build a great plan, get some help. Get a strong coach to come in and help you.

• • •

Once you finish your annual plan, it's time to create your execution plan for the first quarter. The next chapter will show you how to have a great year by planning for a great quarter every quarter.

Bottom Line

Create an annual plan that is inspiring and practical—one that people connect to with their hearts and their heads—to push your strategy forward every year.

→ Develop a main focus. Use a destination postcard and the Time Machine Exercise to describe how the year will be a memorable one in the history of your company. Envision what the year will look like and brainstorm ideas to make it successful.

→ Execute with focus. Once you have your main focus, limit yourself to no more than five initiatives for the year.

→ Execute with purpose. Test your ideas for the year against the company's purpose, BHAG, and winning moves.

→ Discuss, debate, and agree. Achieve clarity while allowing teammates to feel heard. Use the discuss, debate, agree method to gain understanding on issues as you make decisions. The process helps everyone on the team commit to final decisions about the plan.

→ Create a flyover plan. Make your inspiring plan practical. Create a four-quarter flyover plan to look at what needs to be accomplished each quarter to achieve the annual plan.

→ Overcommunicate. Don't keep your plan a secret. Help departments create annual plans of their own and then have an annual kickoff for the whole company.

→ Connect the dots. Help employees connect with the plan by considering these questions: What does it mean to me? How can I help?

CHAPTER 7

EVERY QUARTER
IS A 13-WEEK RACE

*A good plan violently executed now is better
than a perfect plan executed next week.*

—General George Patton

Every quarter is a thirteen-week race. It goes by fast. Before you know
it, the quarter is over. And then the year is over. You are left with the
question, "Did we accomplish what we set out to accomplish?"

To win the thirteen-week race, you need to do two things: (1) You
need a plan for the quarter that your team is excited to execute and
that maps a clear course to achieving critical goals—for the company,
for departments, and for individuals. That is how your teams become
focused and aligned. (2) Get out of their way. Don't distract them during the quarter with unplanned priorities or the next great idea. Do
these two things and you will win your thirteen-week race.

Give your teams what they need to win.

The idea of spending two days to create execution plans every
quarter might make you say, "No way. That is just too much time."
Many of our clients felt the same when we first recommended that
they plan every quarter. But those who implement the rhythm stay

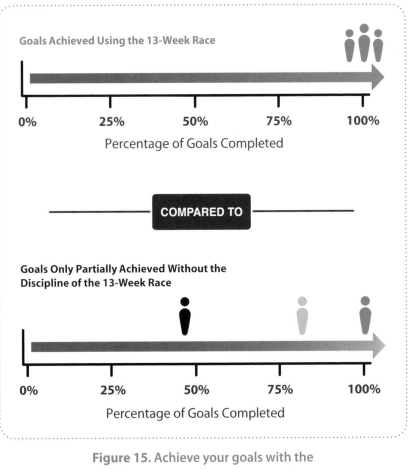

Figure 15. Achieve your goals with the
discipline of a thirteen-week race.

with it because it helps them increase the speed of execution while reducing waste. Imagine if you were able to use the concept of a thirteen-week race to focus and improve your company in one significant way each quarter. You would have improved the company in four significant ways over the course of the year.

As you approach a potential ceiling of complexity, it is easy to lose your focus and for communication to become less effective. With a consistent quarterly Plan Rhythm, you keep your focus, battle poor communication, and break right through the ceiling.

Dutch Valley is a wholesale distributor of bulk foods. When they started working with us, they did not create execution plans each quarter. They only planned for the year, which is a traditional approach to business planning. Matt Burkholder, President and CEO, shared that the shift to planning quarterly rather than just annually made it much easier for them to focus on a few things at a time. "We were doing too much. We were saying, 'Wait, if we don't do this *this* year, it's going to be a whole year before we can get back to it.' Now, we're only planning for thirteen weeks, so if we don't get to it now, we might in thirteen weeks." And that makes it easier to say no—or, maybe later. And that brings focus and alignment. Using the rhythm to make adjustments has been equally powerful. "The process forces you to reevaluate where you are every thirteen weeks, which is really cool." Dutch Valley continues to grow and improve their discipline in how they execute their Plan Rhythm. The company continues to make great progress.

Having a clear plan that every member of the team can align with and be held accountable to creates mutual respect, reduces drama, and builds an atmosphere of helping each other solve problems and adjust during the quarter. Get into a rhythm of coming together as a team every quarter to plan and then cascading that plan throughout the company. Keep your teams on track to have a great year.

5 Steps to Developing a Strong Plan

Your plan of execution for the quarter should consist of the following steps:

1. **Have a main thing.** What is your singular focus for the quarter? Just as you did in your annual plan, work to get your entire com-

pany aligned to accomplish a main thing each quarter. For the quarter, I want you to think in terms of specific results.

2. **Develop three to five company priorities.** What are the three to five priorities that the company needs to accomplish for the quarter? Each of these priorities will be owned by a member of the executive team.

3. **Develop three to five executive team member priorities.** What are the three to five priorities for each executive team member that will support the company priorities?

4. **Develop three to five priorities for every department.** Most of the executive team members' priorities tend to become priorities for their teams or departments to achieve. Each department should consider these and determine which other priorities need to be achieved to support the company's priorities.

5. **Develop three to five priorities for every employee.** Every person in the company should have one or two priorities that are aligned with the department and company priorities for the quarter. The remaining priorities should be used to focus on getting their day jobs done.

Focus discussions on how you will move forward, not on why you are where you are. Information about how you got here should be used only to help you make good decisions. You might have three or four important topics to discuss and reach agreement on each quarter. The preparation by each team member and the strategic thinking should make it clear what discussions you should be having. If you focus your meetings on having these discussions, your plan for the quarter—the main thing and your three to five priorities—gets pretty clear.

When conversations get off track, remind the team why you are there. The purpose of the quarterly plan is to drive your annual plan and your strategy forward. If the conversation is not helping you do that, move on.

RHYTHM EXPERT TIP

"How do I limit my priorities to only five?" Think about sequencing. A quarter is only thirteen weeks. These thirteen weeks will fly by. Use it to really focus on your most important priority. Then ask what you can save for next quarter. The secret is in sequencing your priorities and focusing on fewer things over multiple quarters.

Adjust to Keep Your Annual Plan on Track

Review the quarter that is ending against your plan for the year. Are you on track to have the great year that you visualized in your destination postcard? If yes, celebrate. If no, have a drink anyway and make the necessary adjustment as you plan the new quarter.

Not long ago, I attended a quarterly planning session at Veeam. They had a big revenue goal for the year, and while trying to hit the revenue goal, they found themselves facing a tough question: Should the sales team be focusing more on larger deals with fewer new customers or on smaller deals with more new customers? This was an important question, and it required serious discussion. Each effort required different types of support for the sales team but also a different perspective on the company's approach to sales. Not everybody agreed on the right path, and so the executive team discussed, debated, and eventually came to agree that the goal of the company was to go after a larger number of net new clients—more customers rather than bigger deals. Why? Because the team had already established revenue goals for the next five years, too, and the CEO pointed out that larger deals with bigger numbers might help them get to their current revenue goal, but to achieve their revenue goal for the following year, they needed more customers buying more services. They made an adjustment for the coming quarter that would keep them aligned short-term and long-term.

If you don't make progress toward your annual goals every single quarter, you will have a lousy year. On the other hand, one great quarter after another leads to a great year. Making adjustments and planning to ensure that happens is the purpose of your quarterly Plan Rhythm session.

The Power of Having a Main Thing

When Hostopia brings on a new wholesale customer, such as a telecom company, they have to move thousands of websites from their new customer's servers onto their own. Each website move is called a migration. Migrations are the crux of their business. If they cannot do it efficiently and accurately, they will lose revenues and customers.

When I first started working with Colin Campbell, Hostopia was completing about eight thousand migrations a quarter. The company's growth was dependent on increasing their wholesale clients, so they had to systematically increase their ability to do more migrations and to do them accurately. To increase their capacity and capability, they set a quarterly target of migrating fifteen thousand websites. This was almost twice their best rate.

That goal became their main thing for the quarter. It cascaded down through the company. The team built a plan for an organization—the staff and processes—that could deliver on those fifteen thousand migrations. They hired more people, found vendors to support them, and put in more systems to automate anything that could be. The team members worked extra hours and did whatever it took to make fifteen thousand migrations happen.

They hit the number and celebrated! But when the next quarter came around, the executives had to go back to their teams and say, "Hey guys, we have to do another fifteen thousand migrations this quarter." The employees didn't run screaming from the building because fifteen thousand had become an easy number to hit. They had stretched the capabilities of the organization and created a "new normal." Each quarter after that, they built better systems to manage the migrations. They developed better checks and double-checks. Their migration capability became *the best* in the industry. And guess what? A year later, they did close to *eighty thousand* website migrations in a quarter. Ten times the migrations they were doing a year before!

And it all started with one quarter, when they started a rhythm of stretching their website migration capabilities by focusing on that as a main thing.

Start with the main thing for the quarter. The four-quarter flyover plan, if you have one, could make the main thing for the quarter clear. Ask, is this still true? If you're planning for the first quarter, it probably is, because the annual plan just got done. If you're planning for a later quarter, maybe your flyover plan can guide you, but you must be aware of other things life has brought your way. Life happens. Stuff happens. Plans change. That's why we focus on creating detailed execution plans every quarter. If you have a few candidates for the main focus of the quarter, then discuss, debate, and agree until you feel confident in your main goal.

When your plan is finalized, take your main thing and transform it into a daily question that you can use every day to maintain focus. For example, if the company's main thing this quarter is to "Break barriers for marketing and sales," then a good daily question to ask is "What am I doing today to break barriers for marketing and sales?"

RHYTHM EXPERT TIP

When your plan is finalized, take your main thing and transform it into a daily question that you can use every day to maintain focus.

Commit to the Most Important Priorities

Make a list of potential company priorities that support the main thing for the quarter, the annual plan, and the core business. Use the discuss, debate, agree process to refine the list to three to five quarterly priorities for the company.

Once the three to five company priorities for the quarter have been set, each of the executive or management team members needs to establish individual priorities and share them with the team. Take thirty minutes for each member to work on his or her priorities. A couple of priorities should be pushing the main thing forward, and a couple should be focused on the person's day job. We cannot forget to devote energy to our day jobs! Typically about 80 percent of each executive team member's priorities also translate to departmental priorities. If the leader's priorities match up with the company priorities and are also supported by the department priorities, then you have achieved alignment!

Take the time to have each person share their priorities. Allow them to share how they plan to achieve each priority. What milestones should they achieve along the way? Other executives should be looking for opportunities to assist. You are probably thinking that you can't possibly find the time to help other team members with their priorities. I get it. You have an overflowing plate. But most priorities do not get accomplished by one person or one team. You are looking for opportunities to assist because at some point you will probably be *required to assist*. Better to know that before the quarter starts than to discover it midway through the quarter. These discussions help you test for hidden priorities in the plan. It is much wiser to discuss your availability to assist now rather than disappoint your team later on.

Let's make sure that the priorities we have signed up for do not conflict or compete for the same resources. This is a critical step in the process because to be fully aligned, you need to understand how each other's priorities may affect another team member's priorities, and vice versa.

You cannot plan in silos. We get things done faster and more efficiently when our priorities are complementary. For instance, if one of the priorities of the sales leader is running a new program that requires a different type of client-data-capture system, the IT leader better have developing that system as one of his priorities. If he says that he can't make that a priority because he has others that are taking up all of his resources, the team has to discuss this breakdown in resource allocation, debate the various priorities, and come to agreement on which priorities they will move forward.

You cannot plan in silos. We get things done faster and more efficiently when our priorities are complementary.

Don't walk out of the room

until the priorities of each leader

are understood and agreed

to by the entire team.

And don't accept anything less

than complete commitment.

Respect the plan. Agree that what does not get planned does not get done. Anything else that pops up during the quarter should be put in a parking lot for discussion at the next quarterly planning session. Of course, if you have a crisis or emergency, you need to solve that problem during the quarter. But don't allow false emergencies to distract you from the plan. Respecting the plan during the quarter causes the team to deepen their commitment at the next planning session. Conversely, if you do not respect the plan during the quarter, your team will believe that the planning session was a waste of time and have less of a commitment to this process.

These are the right discussions to be having. Don't walk out of the room until the priorities of each leader are understood and agreed to by the entire team. And don't accept anything less than complete commitment.

Make Sure Your Plan Is "Execution Ready"

The main thing and the priorities for the company and the executive team members are the critical elements of your quarterly plan. However, the plan is not complete until you have tested it and developed the tools you need to support it. If you do not have a complete plan, people cannot execute it or make adjustments to keep it on track. Before you run off and start executing an incomplete plan, discuss it further to make sure it is strong and will get you where you want to go. If your plan fails any of the four tests below, fix it!

→ **Financial Test:** Does the plan achieve the company's financial goals? It is possible to have a plan that does not achieve the company's financial goals. I call this an insufficient plan. Take a step back and make sure that the priorities the team has chosen will indeed achieve the overall financial goals. And if not, work to fully understand what is missing from the plan.

→ **Focus Test:** Do you have a main focus that everyone supports? Is it clear what you are supposed to achieve this quarter?

→ **Energy Test:** Is there enough energy—priorities—focused on the company's main thing? If not, then your team is not well aligned to run this thirteen-week race together.

→ **Accountability Test:** Do all priorities (company, executive, department, and individual) have clear success criteria? Your plan is not complete until you have clear and objective success criteria. Without them, it is impossible to create drama-free accountability. Even more crucial, without this success criteria, it will be very hard to make adjustments throughout the quarter. I will discuss success criteria in more detail in the next chapter.

Jill, a CEO client, shared with me that her team was not achieving their main thing for the quarter. I applied the Energy Test to her plan. We discovered that hardly anyone on the team was working on it! How could that be? It was an unfortunate case of everyone thinking that someone else was working on it, so no one was working on it. Learning from this painful lesson, Jill started applying the four tests to her plan moving forward. She had tons of energy applied to the company's main thing the next quarter. It was a much more successful quarter.

Once you are sure your company plan is solid, you want to be able to use it well every day. That means cascading it to build department and individual plans.

Get Fully Aligned With Your Departments

We hire managers to make our lives easier, yet sometimes, with every new manager we hire, we often feel as if we have more work, not less. If you are feeling this way, that means you have not allowed your managers to manage their teams. Let go. Allow your managers to be the wind in your sails. Believe me, your managers are waiting for that day. They want more responsibility, and they want to be more involved in establishing the direction of their departments.

Your execution really takes off when you involve the next level of managers and everyone else in your execution planning. It's the process of planning together rather than dictating a plan from the top down that helps get everyone aligned and committed to executing the plan. When you are a smaller company, everyone wears multiple hats. As you grow, each role tends to become more specialized. Now you need to involve others in your execution planning. Thinking goes from "me" to "we." It's no longer "What I'm doing to move the company forward." It's now "What are we doing to move the company forward?" People don't choose to be misaligned on purpose. It just happens. That is why you need a planning process that involves everybody. It encourages people to collectively move the company forward. Without that collective mindset, you won't be able to grow efficiently. Yet many growth companies zoom right past the "Cascade your plan with your team" sign without noticing it. It happens rather suddenly, and unless you are watchful and very aware, you lose alignment and effectiveness down the ranks of your company.

Your execution really takes off when you involve the next level of managers and everyone else in your execution planning.

Simms Fishing, the leader in the fly-fishing market that I first mentioned in part 1, is 130-employees strong with four functional areas—product development, operations, sales and marketing, and finance and accounting—and multiple departments in each of those areas. Five years ago, the heads of those departments would have put communication at the top of their company issues list. But not anymore. These days, they get all of the information they could want or need.

Every quarter, after the executive team meets for two days to come up with their quarterly plan, they meet with the greater management team, including directors, managers, and supervisors. They go over the game plan for the quarter and they ask for feedback from all of the team members. Then the team leaders get together in their functional groups for planning sessions, where they create priorities for the departments that relate to the key priorities for the company. In fact, every person in the company is involved in the quarterly planning process in some way.

K.C. shared, "Rhythm planning and reporting is second nature to Simms at this point. Internal communication and clarity around our annual and quarterly plans throughout our organization is no longer an issue. It's impossible to imagine how we would have grown these last five years without Rhythm and the coaching that we receive from Rhythm Systems."

RHYTHM EXPERT TIP

Let your executive team learn and grow in confidence over one or two quarters before rolling the planning rhythm out to departments and other teams.

• • •

What does a strong cascade planning process offer? Limited silos, reduced cross-department tension, and elimination of unclear directives and confusion among frontline employees about where to direct their energy. Quarter after quarter, your teams will be aligned and successful. They will be more productive. Chris Tinsley, Chief Technology Officer for AvidXchange, saw an incredible boost in productivity when they began cascading the planning process to every employee in the company. They had been tracking productivity through what they called the velocity metric for a couple of years. For 2012, they established a specific goal to hit. They began to cascade the quarterly plans in the first quarter of 2012, and by the third quarter, the R&D team had increased their productivity by 300 percent! "We always talk about what the quarterly objectives are and we roll those all the way down to the coders who are writing code, the QA people who are testing the code, the tech ops who are keeping the software up and running. We're able to tie all of their priorities together so that they can see

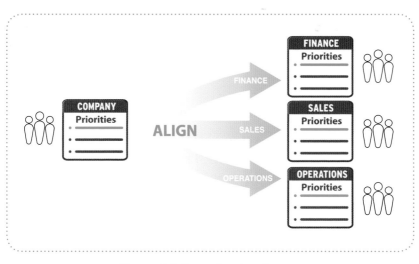

Figure 16. Cascade planning to departments, teams, and individuals.

how they contribute to the quarterly priorities for the department and the company."

To execute with speed, cascade plans and priorities to departments, teams, and individuals.

Creating Department Plans

When cascading to departments and teams, it is best to be clear on what results the company is working toward, to share the plan that the executive team created to achieve those results, and to ask everyone to work on an execution plan to deliver on their part of those results. Don't micromanage the departments. Share the result, the "what" to achieve, and allow them to focus on the "how." How will they contribute to achieving the overall plan? Planning at the department level gives every department clarity and alignment with the company's overall efforts. It eliminates the communication gap.

Follow these steps to cascade your planning process to departments:

1. **Communicate.** Share the company plan with every department.

2. **Plan.** Every executive team member should lead his or her department to develop their own execution plan.

3. **Confirm.** Confirm your plans with other departments. Don't plan in silos.

Executives should spend a half day to develop execution plans with their departments. Then, to avoid planning in silos, have all department heads meet and share their plans with each other. Take the opportunity to discuss, debate, and agree until the department heads are aligned on priorities and milestones for each priority throughout the quarter. Let people raise their concerns about resources. Let them point out conflicts. Let them say, "If you want my team member to do this for you, the other project you wanted to get done can't get done. You have to choose." This is when you make the tough choices. You have to ask, what trade-offs will we have to make in order to focus on these specific priorities?

When everybody signs off on their plan for the quarter, there shouldn't be any question as to what each department is going to do to make the company's main thing happen.

Cascade your planning process to your departments and to all employees. Until you do, you don't actually have a plan.

Develop Individual Priorities That Move Your Plan Forward

When you reach about seventy-five people in your organization, it becomes harder to get everyone at all levels of the company to understand how they personally impact the company. But when everyone understands how their own priorities connect to company plans and strategies, it creates excitement and gets everyone at all levels of the company engaged.

Once department plans are set, department leaders should work with their teams to develop individual priorities that support the plan. All employees should have one personal priority focused on helping the company move its plan forward. The other remaining personal priorities should be focused on achieving their day jobs. The manager follows the same process that was followed at the cascade meeting, beginning with presenting the department plan to the team. Then the team members develop their personal priorities and share them with the team to create alignment within the department.

When every employee in the company has a set of priorities for the quarter that align up and down the organization, you will achieve absolute alignment. Now everyone understands how they personally impact the company.

• • •

There is no excuse for not having a plan for your quarter. Moving the organization forward is always better than not moving forward. Use the quarterly planning process to give your teams the focus they need to win the thirteen-week race every quarter. That is the key to growth.

Bottom Line

To win the thirteen-week race that happens every quarter, you need a detailed execution plan that drives your annual plan forward.

→ Plan a two-day execution-planning session every quarter before the quarter begins. Do it now.

→ During your Plan Rhythm session, create a quarterly plan with a main thing or point of focus for the quarter, three to five company priorities, and three to five priorities for each executive team member.

→ To help you get to a great plan, have a slate of important topics ready for discussion during your planning session.

→ Review your quarter for necessary adjustments to keep you on track for the annual destination.

→ Create a main thing that brings focus to every person's work for the quarter. Use a "daily question" to drive your main thing during your thirteen-week race.

→ Create priorities for the company and the executives that are aligned. The executive team members' priorities should support the company priorities and should also reflect their department priorities.

→ Spend time sharing and discussing priorities and looking for opportunities to assist. Test the plan for hidden priorities—those that will crop up in the middle of the quarter, requiring you to devote your resources to help somebody else achieve a priority.

→ Test your plan with the four tests: Financial Test, Focus Test, Energy Test, and Accountability Test.

→ Cascade your planning process to your departments and to all employees. Until you do, you don't actually have a plan. Cascading your plan closes the communication gap and creates clear priorities for every person in the organization for the quarter.

→ Get your day jobs done! Frontline employees should only have one priority that drives the company plan forward. The rest of their energy should be focused on achieving their ongoing day jobs.

CHAPTER 8

THE POWER OF LEADING INDICATORS AND DASHBOARDS

It is no use saying, "We are doing our best"
You have got to succeed in doing what is necessary.

—Winston Churchill

When Don Fraynd of Chicago Public Schools first contacted us, I wondered, *How can we help a public school system?* But as I learned about Don's purpose, I became excited. Our work could improve the lives of thousands of children!

Don Fraynd was the head of the Office of School Improvement (OSI) for Chicago Public Schools. Their mission? Whole-school turn-arounds for the lowest-performing schools in the district—schools that were in the bottom 5 percent. Chicago was one of the first school districts in the country to attempt this. These schools had seen other reform initiatives come and go over the years, mostly outsourced to the private sector. Don described it as throwing jelly at the wall. When one program didn't stick, they tried another. OSI's mission was to create a plan that was integrated with the public school system and that would overcome past mistakes in school reform to create sustainable growth in performance. Don was not responsible for marginal schools.

He was responsible for turning around some of the very worst high schools in the country, where three or four kids a year were shot and killed in the neighborhood, primarily on nights and weekends. He had to help students who were parentless or homeless focus on college preparedness skills.

OSI was halfway through their first year at their third turnaround school, John Marshall Metropolitan High School, the subject of the movie *Hoop Dreams*. They had learned from the bright spots and the adjustments made in their first two schools. Over time, Don had established five key performance indicators (KPIs)—two results indicators and three leading indicators—to keep his team on track with the plan. OSI's results indicators were (1) grades and test scores and (2) graduation rates. Their leading indicators were (1) attendance, (2) misconduct, and (3) freshmen on track to graduate. These leading indicators would help them make sure they were on track to achieve the results they were striving for. If attendance was low and misconduct was high, how could they improve grades or test scores? And if they could determine early on, from the very first year, if they were preparing kids to graduate, then they could improve graduation rates down the line.

We helped OSI improve how they used these KPIs by applying the right success criteria and publishing them in dashboards that were cascaded throughout the schools. The leading indicators, success criteria, and dashboards connected metrics to action for everybody in the schools. "We realized that adults were not the only ones that could benefit from seeing their data displayed publicly and prominently," explained Don. "So we actually tasked a position in our building— the activities director—with publishing the dashboard for the school publicly, but also to use metric challenges for different groups of kids. So we had sophomores versus freshmen in terms of attendance improvement. We used data to inspire them to improve their behavior, improve attendance, grow their grades, etcetera." And they used dashboards with their vendors, like after-school-program providers. If a vendor couldn't show how their programs were improving the primary KPIs, Don and the principals ended their contract and worked with a vendor that could show improvement.

This was truly amazing! Not only did Don cascade KPIs and success criteria to departments, he cascaded them to vendors! This created tremendous focus, alignment, and accountability while helping the school achieve the results that they wanted.

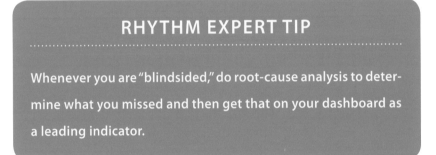

RHYTHM EXPERT TIP

Whenever you are "blindsided," do root-cause analysis to determine what you missed and then get that on your dashboard as a leading indicator.

By the end of their first year with Marshall, the leading indicators told the true story: Average daily attendance had gone from 53 percent to 75 percent. Only 2.5 percent of students had met or exceeded state proficiency exams in the 2010 school year. That increased to 5.1

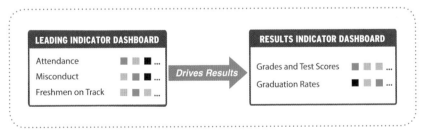

Figure 17. Focus on leading indicators to produce future results.

Leading indicators tell you the story that is about to be written. What it might be, when you still have the power to change the story.

percent the first year of the turnaround—a strong improvement. Their "freshmen on track"—those on track to graduate—had increased to 70 percent from 30 percent the previous year. With every percentage improvement they save more children. They save more lives.

• • •

In the introduction, I told you about my Jerry Maguire moment. Out of that moment came an insight that changed how I have viewed management and execution ever since: It's really about using the right leading indicators to help you make the right adjustments. Most of us are looking at results indicators. Results indicators are good and necessary. They tell you the story of what has already happened. What you have already achieved. However, leading indicators tell you the story that is about to be written. What it might be, when you still have the power to change the story. Just like Don of CPS, if you have a few leading indicators, you have that much more power to drive the results you want. Dashboards built on leading indicators and a red-yellow-green approach to measuring progress can help any organization execute better. They can help you become more team centric, candid, and results oriented. They can help you build accountability, individually and collectively, and promote self-management. I am not knocking results indicators. You need them. You just have to realize that they report on what has already happened. You don't need leading indicators instead of results indicators. Rather, you need both. It is the power of the A-N-D. Use both results and leading indicators to help you achieve the right results.

No execution plan is complete until you have the right few KPIs, success criteria, and dashboards in place.

You don't need leading indicators instead of results indicators.

Rather, you need both.

It's the power of the A-N-D.

4 Steps to Developing Leading Indicators

Leading indicators are the KPIs that can give you some insight as to what is about to happen. They are predictive. They help you peer around the corner. Leading indicators are future focused. Accountability to the right leading indicators with clear success criteria will drive performance.

How do you develop and use leading indicators? Here is a four-step process to help you.

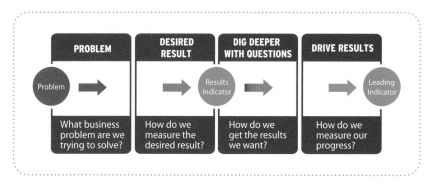

Figure 18. Four-step process to develop leading indicators

→ **Step 1: Identify the problem.** Begin with the end in mind. What is your goal, or what business problem are you trying to solve?

→ **Step 2: Clarify the desired result.** What is your desired outcome? What results would you like to achieve? Think of your results in measurable terms, like percentage of growth. This is your results indicator.

→ **Step 3: Dig deeper with questions.** Ask questions about what drives and creates the results that you are looking for. You are going to have to dig deep by asking questions. Sometimes it takes five or six questions to get to the best leading indicator to drive the results that you are looking for.

→ **Step 4: Drive results.** What is the best leading indicator to drive the results that you want? What do we push on and how do we measure our progress? What are the red-yellow-green success criteria for your leading indicator?

How do you know when you have found a leading indicator? It is measurable, and you can influence it or push on it for results. Recall

Rhythm™ Growth Tools	Leading Indicator Creator

What Business Problem are we trying to solve?

1	What is your Main Business Problem?		2	Desired Outcome	When

How will we measure the RESULTS?

3	Result Indicator (KPI)	Success Criteria	
			SG
			Green
		between Green and Red	Yellow
			Red

What is the LEADING Indicator that helps us drive toward achieving the Results?

4	Leading Indicator (KPI)	Success Criteria	
			SG
			Green
		between Green and Red	Yellow
			Red

Test your Leading Indicator

5	Test	Y/N
	Does your Leading Indicator predict the right results?	
	Is it within your control? Can you influence your Leading Indicator?	

OSI's leading indicators: freshmen on track to graduate, attendance, and misconduct. If they could improve in those areas, graduation rates and test scores and grades would improve. They could easily measure attendance and misconduct, and they developed a method for measuring freshmen on track.

Many times we have seen executives stop after asking two or three questions. They stop just before true insight is uncovered. Don't stop asking questions until you discover a strong leading indicator to help you solve your particular business problem.

RHYTHM EXPERT TIP

Eliminate weak indicators by asking why until you think you'll cry. Asking why five times is about right. Many clients stop just short of a strong leading indicator. The best executive teams stay focused on indicators that support good decisions; e.g., I taught my son to look beyond the car in front for red brake lights. It's a good leading indicator that the car in front of you will begin to brake, too. A business decision made a fraction of a second early can be the difference between a successful journey and an accident.

• • •

White Lodging is a $1 billion company that operates more than 170 hotels for premium brands like Marriott, Hilton, Hyatt, and a number of others. When we first started working with them, they wanted to focus on improving operations across all properties. The goal was to create a consistent and ever-improving guest experience that would help the company double in growth in five years. Early on in our work, we shared with the leaders that most of the metrics they were tracking were lagging indicators. They didn't have many indicators to help them know if they were on track for future success. So for each of the four drivers of their success, they asked, "What can we measure that will help us know if we're heading toward a train wreck?" Today, White Lodging has a dashboard with four leading indicators for each hotel. But they also have used leading indicators to help them make progress on their results.

For instance, one of the drivers of success at a hotel is the speed with which an open general-manager position is filled. If a GM position is open for more than forty-five days, the hotel starts to deteriorate pretty quickly, in all areas. Unfortunately, they were filling open positions in fewer than forty-five days less than 62 percent of the time. So they asked the right question: "What drives getting a GM position filled in fewer than forty-five days?" After asking more questions, they discovered the leading indicator was having a virtual bench of candidates ready and waiting—candidates who were genuinely interested in working at White Lodging, who had passed the initial screening tests, and who were potentially prepared to accept the position if they were offered the job after a rigorous interviewing process. Guess how many people they had in their virtual bench for GM positions? Zero!

So the executive team made filling GM positions quickly a priority. If it was a driver of hotel success, it needed to be. They worked on their virtual bench, they refined their interview process to prequalify candidates, and in just eighteen months, they moved that 62 percent to 84 percent! Imagine how many train wrecks they are avoiding by being proactive. They can be proactive because what they measure is a leading indicator that prompts them to take action before the potential crisis arrives.

Here are a few tips for using your leading indicators to achieve strong results:

→ **Share your KPIs.** Go public with them. Don't be afraid to educate other teams and ask them how they can positively impact your KPIs. This is how you get other teams aligned with you.

→ **Measure what you want to move, instead of measuring everything that moves.** Measure only the most important few KPIs to give people the right focus. Most people make the mistake of having too many KPIs to keep track of. And to top it off, when I ask what actions are taken for specific KPIs, I get that glazed look. You don't need that many KPIs. You only need a few if you actually take action. Everything else is waste!

→ **Identify a critical number to measure your progress for each quarter and each year.** For the year, your critical number may be a key financial, such as revenue or revenue growth. You should also find a way to measure your progress on the main thing for the quarter. Develop a leading indicator and make that your critical number for the quarter. Track your critical number and discuss it weekly with your team.

After you have discovered your KPIs, use them to create accountability and drive the right actions. It is action that helps you get results. To guide the hard work of your teams, establish red-yellow-green (RYG) success criteria.

RHYTHM EXPERT TIP

One client changed their leading indicator from "revenue" to "A+ customers in the sales pipeline." This one change focused them on the quality of their sales pipeline, instead of the quantity of prospects in their sales pipeline. This change helped them to shore up sales for the year, and it put them in a great position to expect record growth in the following year.

Red-Yellow-Green: The Power of Having Clear Success Criteria

For every KPI and priority, you must have clear success criteria in order to track your progress. When discussing progress, you need to be able to ask, "As compared to what?" As compared to the success criteria that we agreed on up front! If you establish leading indicators for the critical priorities of your annual and quarterly plan, it is the comparison to prior established success criteria that will tell if you are on track or if you need to make an adjustment. Good success criteria help you quickly communicate your progress to the entire team. Red-yellow-green is a simple approach that helps you to do this.

Think of assigning RYG criteria to your KPIs and priorities like this:

→ **Green:** This is the goal. This is how you describe success.

→ **Red:** This is failure. If the goal or KPI comes in at red at the end of the quarter, we have failed as a team on this goal.

→ **Yellow:** Yellow is between red and green.

→ **SuperGreen™:** And then there is SuperGreen! SuperGreen is the stretch goal.

SuperGreen is important because many ambitious executives set targets that are really stretch goals, and their teams do not believe they are achievable. When your team does not believe the target is achievable, you have already lost before beginning your race.

I received a call from a friend: Jack, a CEO. He wanted some help because his sales team was not achieving quota. To top it off, performance was getting worse, even though the sales quota was well set and extremely clear. He was not quite sure what to do. Jack figured that he had a problem with one of the three Ps—people, process, product—but he was not sure which. When I interviewed his sales team, I discovered that no one had ever achieved the sales quota, including the top salesperson. When I shared this insight with Jack, he replied, "Of course! If the quota is too low, that would be too easy. You've always said that if you aim for the sky and hit the trees, it's okay. But if you aim for the trees and hit the dirt, no one is happy! So I am aiming for the skies and hitting the trees." This was a classic example of an ambitious CEO who wanted to set ambitious goals. Unfortunately, his stretch goal was demoralizing the troops. Jack had to reset his success criteria. Once he used RYG and SuperGreen correctly, his sales team stopped freaking out and got productive.

The Process for Red-Yellow-Green

Red-yellow-green is simple, and it seems easy. But executives need to slow down and discuss what success really looks like and how to measure it in order to execute faster during the quarter. If you don't do this work, you won't be able to describe success clearly. Lack of clarity will lead to drama during the quarter when you try to hold people accountable.

Here is how you develop great RYG metrics. Let's use achieving a sales goal of $1 million as an example:

→ **Step 1: Set your green criteria.** We would like to achieve $1 million in sales. So green = $1 million in sales closed.

→ **Step 2: Determine what red is.** What is the minimum level of sales we need to achieve to keep our plan on track? What level of sales would force us to reconsider our budgets for the year? This would be the red criteria. Achieving sales less than this number may require the company to change the plan for the rest of the year. And if the goal is to achieve a quarterly plan that supports the annual plan, this is a bad thing. A sales number in the red range has negative consequences for the entire year. In this example, let's say that number is anything less than $700,000, which would be the red criteria.

→ **Step 3: Determine what yellow is.** Yellow is between red and green, so between $700,000 and $1 million.

→ **Step 4: Determine what SuperGreen is.** What is our stretch goal? What would motivate your ambitious A players? Your stretch goal is the SuperGreen criteria. For this example, let's say that number is $1.25 million and above.

In this example, sales would probably be a KPI for the company. I am also often asked how to establish red-yellow-green criteria for priorities, especially priorities that don't seem to be number based. The question to ask is, if you are to achieve the goal or accomplish the priority, what needs to happen along the way? The answer to this question may be a number you can track weekly. For example, if the priority is an individual's sales goal, the driver might be the number of sales calls each week or a progression of projected revenue. Or the answer may be a series of milestones with completion dates. For each week, you status red, yellow, or green based on whether you think a milestone will be completed on time. So the RYG criteria for the first three weeks of a quarter might be based on one milestone, the next three weeks based on the next milestone, and so on. The important thing is to be very specific about what it is that's going to be accomplished.

Slowing down to discuss success in this way will help the team think through what it takes to succeed. Consider what actions you might want to take if this goal falls into the yellow or red zone during the quarter. Talk about it now before it happens, when you are calm and can think clearly. Do not wait until you are facing a crisis to decide what corrective actions you might consider.

RHYTHM EXPERT TIP

Start using red-yellow-green language today. Recently, a new client created RYG status codes for their long-used data spreadsheet. In four weeks they moved team conversations from "What's wrong?" (or "Who's wrong?") to "How can we make adjustments?" That's the power of using RYG!

The Gift of Red

I have found red to be a very powerful part of this exercise that many people miss. If the team has discussed what red is, what it means to the company, and what corrective actions may be necessary, red can drive performance and eliminate a lot of drama during the quarter. It is the minimum performance discussed and agreed upon as a team. Here's the key. If you establish red criteria up front, and everyone knows what it is and understands the impact to the company, you will have a strong team. The team will help each other work on solutions and navigate away from red. They will respond positively and work on solutions for priorities and KPIs that are in danger of falling into the red zone. We will discuss the power of making the right adjustments in part 3. Without red, you lose the urgency of coming up with solutions to make the right adjustments.

I often stress that it is the priority or KPI that is red, not the person. Focusing on the priority and solutions needed instead of focusing on the people is what allows teams to work together and help each other get the priority or KPI from red back to green.

How to Use Dashboards to Drive Results

A dashboard is the perfect tool to help you communicate progress throughout the company and hold people accountable while preserving relationships. Use dashboards as helpful and actionable tools, not to club people on the head, and you will speed up your execution and reduce mistakes. They should be used to identify problems that need to be solved and to gather real insights about the company's progress. So 90 percent of the success of dashboards is determining what should go into them and how your team will use them to solve problems collaboratively.

If you are not tracking your progress every week on your KPIs and priorities, how do you know if you are making progress on the right things? As part of your Plan Rhythm, you should develop the following thirteen-week dashboards that can be easily updated every week.

→ **Company dashboard:** A dashboard displaying the company's top two KPIs and top three to five priorities

→ **Department dashboard:** A dashboard displaying the department's top two KPIs and top three to five priorities

→ **Personal dashboards:** A dashboard displaying each person's top two KPIs and top three to five priorities

These dashboards should be shared, not hidden. Post dashboards publicly every week. This simple step speeds growth by promoting transparency and candid conversations. They get entire teams focused on solving problems. Tap into the collective intelligence of your teams and get more done with less! Remember, the purpose of tracking RYG success criteria with dashboards isn't to beat people up about being off track. We will discuss how to use dashboards as part of your Do Rhythm in part 3. The purpose is to highlight the need for adjustments so that you can take swift action.

Bottom Line

To make sure you have a successful quarter every quarter, establish leading indicators with clear success criteria and track them publicly on visual dashboards.

→ There are two types of key performance indicators: (1) Results indicators tell you what has happened. (2) Leading indicators predict what will happen in the future. They let you know if you are on track to achieve the results you want.

→ A leading indicator has two characteristics: (1) It is measurable. (2) You can influence and move it. With these two characteristics, you can use leading indicators to drive performance.

→ When searching for your leading indicators, ask why at least five times. Dig deep to find the indicator that can predict as well as drive the right actions and results.

→ Use clear success criteria. The red-yellow-green approach creates clarity and signals your teams to take action when necessary. And don't forget SuperGreen for stretch goals!

→ Create RYG criteria for your priorities as well as your KPIs.

→ Don't be afraid of setting red criteria. It is a gift! When you use red as part of your success criteria, people tend to manage themselves away from it.

→ Create dashboards to drive execution during your thirteen-week race. Use it every single week. Use dashboards to communicate progress throughout the company and create accountability without drama!

PLAN RHYTHM: 14 ACTIONS TO GET YOU GOING

1. If you have not already, complete the Rhythm Assessment at www.PatrickThean.com.

2. Download the Plan Rhythm tools, including the Leading Indicator Creator.

3. If you have not already scheduled your quarterly and annual Rhythm sessions, do so now. Put them on the calendar, alert your team, and make them happen. Yes, schedule two full days for each.

4. Begin planning at the executive team level. Cascading is critical, but don't start it right away. Get good at this rhythm first, and then roll it out to managers and the rest of the company.

5. Discuss, debate, and agree. Make sure that you are reaching actual agreement, not pretend agreement. If everybody on the team does not agree on the path forward, execution will go poorly because you won't be aligned.

6. Develop a communication plan for your annual execution plan. How will you roll it out to the company? How will you get people excited about it? How will you tell the story of what the company's year will look like to engage people's heads and hearts? This is a critical moment in the success of the year. Develop a plan for it so that you get it right. Don't send it out in a memo.

7. When you are ready to begin the cascade process, put it on your schedule. About a week after each quarterly planning session (so that you have time to sleep on your quarterly plan and confirm that it's the right plan) schedule a day or

a half-day session with your team to develop your department execution plan.

8. Don't plan in silos. Share your department plan with all departments as part of your planning process every quarter.

9. Identify a facilitator to make your planning sessions effective and productive. Have the facilitator and each team member review both the tips for having a productive planning session and the process for discuss, debate, agree before each session.

10. Spend the right amount of time identifying the right KPIs, especially leading indicators that help you peer into the future and make adjustments if necessary.

11. Slow down to create strong red-yellow-green success criteria for all priorities and KPIs. Without these elements, your plan is not complete. Clear and concise success criteria will allow you to compare your execution to your plan and make any adjustments necessary to achieve your plan.

12. Create thirteen-week dashboards for each set of priorities that come out of your planning sessions: company, departmental, and personal.

13. Dashboards are critical communication tools that will form the foundation of your Do Rhythm. You may want to begin with a company dashboard only, to help people get used to the idea. You can then cascade the tool down to executive team members, then to departments, and eventually to all employees.

14. Make most dashboards public. Develop a way to make them easily accessible for review. Print them and post them on the walls if necessary.

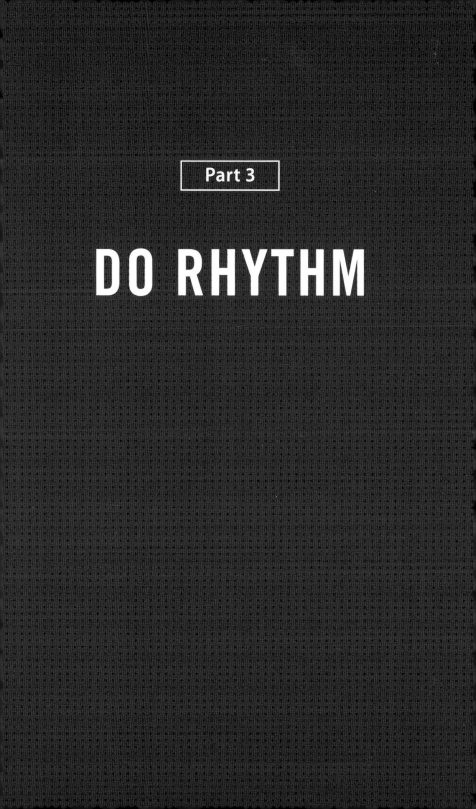

Part 3

DO RHYTHM

CHAPTER 9

NOTHING HAPPENS UNTIL YOU DO THE WORK

By failing to prepare you are preparing to fail.

—Benjamin Franklin

Guest-satisfaction scores. Hotels live and die by them. Hotel management and operating companies like White Lodging even more so. Dave Sibley, CEO of White Lodging Hospitality Management, understood that every hotel's GSS (guest-satisfaction survey) score was a key leading indicator for the success of that hotel. "We know the GSS score is key. But with a hundred and seventy hotels and multiple layers of management, it just seemed like a huge challenge to get everyone focused on it. And we didn't really know if people were taking action quickly when things got off track." Bryan Hayes, their COO, concurred: "We were reporting the GSS scores every week and we thought they were going to get better, but we were not sure exactly what was being done at each hotel to make them better."

They needed a Do Rhythm, a consistent rhythm to systematically review how things were going compared to their plan and to make adjustments to keep the plan on track.

The first thing we did was to help White Lodging convert their weekly meetings from status meetings to Adjustment Meetings. They considered how they were performing according to the plan for the quarter and discussed possible adjustments. Everyone in the weekly meeting was accountable for coming prepared with insights into how they would achieve the goals they had committed to for the quarter. Each team member reviewed the previous week and updated the status of their priorities on their dashboards before the meeting. This focus on achieving the quarterly plan week by week caused the team to become more proactive. Their status meetings became problem-solving meetings.

To improve the effectiveness of their weekly execution, we helped them develop success criteria for their GSS and recognize that it was a leading indicator for revenue growth. Every week, they discussed their critical KPIs, including guest-satisfaction scores, and any adjustments that needed to be made to have a great week, and ultimately, a great quarter. The general managers of the hotels began having weekly regional meetings. They talked about what they could do to improve their KPIs. They learned how their peers were solving problems. The corporate leadership team met and discussed what they could do to improve KPIs across hotels, how they could support the general managers.

Not long ago, this Do Rhythm helped them spot an important adjustment that was necessary for their plan to succeed. Bryan noted that the GSS score had slipped and had a yellow status. At their Weekly Adjustment Meeting, the team came prepared to discuss what solutions they should consider to get back on track. As they peeled back the onion, they realized that it was poor Internet performance that was hurting the GSS score. The head of IT took action. He and his team dug in, learned what the issues were, and made adjustments to significantly improve Internet service for guests.

"Before we implemented Rhythm, that conversation never would have happened until it was a crisis," said Bryan. "Life is very different now. Because we were having these conversations every week, the head of IT realized how he could impact a KPI for my entire division. And now we know exactly what actions to take and who is working to solve that problem!" Crisis averted. GSS went back up. Most important, the Do Rhythm kept their plan on track for the quarter.

The only way to have a great year is to have four great quarters. How do you have a great quarter? By having thirteen great weeks. The Do Rhythm will help you effectively execute your plan. It helps your team practice accountability in a way that allows the right adjustments to achieve the results in your plan.

When we build our plans, we cannot account for every hurdle that might appear in our path. We do not know what we might learn about our priorities in week six of the quarter. We do not know how the business environment might change over the next few months. You can plan all you want. Nothing actually happens until you do the work! And once you start doing the work, you uncover issues you did not plan for. Successful companies are nimble and stay on track to hit their goals for the quarter and year. That is what the Do Rhythm offers you.

You can plan all you want. Nothing actually happens until you do the work!

Do Rhythm: Make Decisions Faster as a Team

To make sure that planning becomes doing, you need a weekly rhythm that focuses your teams on doing the important work. This weekly rhythm keeps your teams focused, aligned, and accountable for achieving your quarterly plan. It consists of a series of meetings and activities designed to help you get work done, make decisions, and move your plan forward faster:

→ **Meeting with Myself:** Spend thirty minutes each week reviewing the week that just ended and setting your priorities for the coming week. Ask yourself what insights you can glean from the week that can help you have a stronger next week.

→ **Weekly Adjustment Meeting:** Meet with the team weekly to realign and focus on achieving the plan for the quarter.

→ **Adjustment Meetings to solve specific problems:** Meet with the right team members to focus and solve a specific problem that has you stuck. These are single-topic meetings. They are focused on discussing and solving one problem.

You might think that this seems like a lot of meetings. However, these meetings defy the traditional concept of meetings. They aren't status meetings or meetings about the work. These are meetings to do the work and make decisions. This is an important shift. You're probably already spending this time having ad hoc discussions and meetings in hallways. But you aren't getting to the most effective decisions efficiently. These meetings allow the members of healthy teams to work together and reach solutions faster than if they were working on their own. You don't have to meet about the work. You meet to *do the work.*

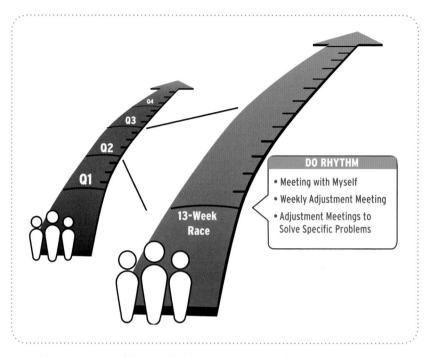

Figure 19. Weekly Do Rhythm to win your thirteen-week race

Bryan Hayes of White Lodging demonstrated how the Do Rhythm promises to equip your team with the ability to prevent fires instead of engaging in firefighting. If you practice this rhythm, you will make adjustments in the fourth, fifth, or sixth week of the quarter instead of fighting the fires of crises in the tenth or eleventh week of the quarter. As managers and leaders, we need to do the hard work of holding our teams accountable for getting the work done. It is our job to inspect what we expect. And it is hard work! The Do Rhythm coupled with dashboards will help you focus your teams and keep them accountable for delivering results.

Everyone Is Accountable to Keep the Plan on Track

When companies are small, it seems natural to do whatever it takes to help the company succeed. Team members contribute to the success of the company regardless of department divisions. But as companies grow, more people join the team and layers of management are added. That all-hands-on-deck culture tends to shift. Team members become singularly focused on getting their jobs done rather than focusing on how their jobs help to move the company's plan forward. Mistakes are blamed on other departments or on "growing pains." This is an early indication that silos are forming inside your company. It happens slowly until one day it seems as though it happened suddenly.

So as we hire more employees, how do we keep everyone engaged in moving the company plan, not just their department plans, forward? The process of planning with departments described in part 2 is one way to prevent silos from developing. Another way is to use your Do Rhythm to focus on moving the company's plan forward together, in all departments. All must hold themselves accountable to achieving their priorities and KPIs and allowing their teammates to help them get unstuck when they are struggling.

Self-accountability is key to an effective Do Rhythm. To build self-accountability in your team, you must be transparent about how the work is coming along. To do this, make sure that you have clear red-yellow-green (RYG) success criteria for every priority and KPI. Then use dashboards as a tool to achieve results. Focus on developing solutions when the status of any KPI or priority turns yellow or red. RYG success criteria and dashboards are the foundation of a process of accountability and adjustments. In part 2 we discussed how to develop these tools. With RYG, we can agree with our teams what success and failure look like for the agreed-upon KPIs and priorities

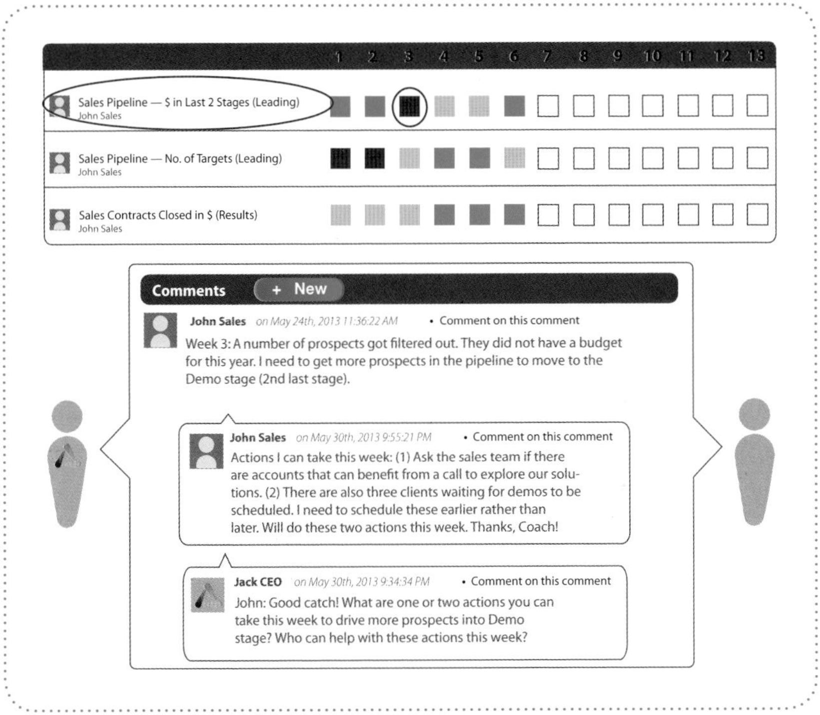

Figure 20. Use dashboards to trigger discussions.
Dashboards do not solve problems. People do!

in an objective way. With dashboards, we communicate status on priorities and KPIs transparently. Combined, the two allow us to have discussions and help each other solve problems.

When I say "accountability," images of gnashing of teeth and whacking of heads typically come to mind. Most of us are natural-born head-whackers. Instead, think about accountability differently. Think about accountability as the process that allows us to compare where we are to the plan so that we can help each other make the right adjustments and succeed. When we do this as soon as we discover a problem, we give ourselves the best chance of having a successful quarter. When you think of dashboards as action-oriented tools for

When you think of dashboards as action-oriented tools for making adjustments, not head-whacking clubs, your teams will catapult to a new level of performance.

making adjustments, not head-whacking clubs, your teams will catapult to a new level of performance.

In her book *Multipliers*, Liz Wiseman shared that multipliers are leaders who "use their intelligence to amplify the smarts and capabilities of the people around them. When these leaders walk into a room, light bulbs go off over people's heads; ideas flow and problems get solved. These are the leaders who inspire employees to stretch themselves to deliver results that surpass expectations."[3] I believe that teaching self-accountability in a low-drama way is one way that leaders become multipliers. And to use these tools to be a multiplier, you need to

1. **Encourage transparency, no matter what.** If it's red, it's red. The faster the team learns it's red, the faster the team can work toward making the adjustments and getting the priority or KPI back into healthy green. When roadblocks arise, encourage people to status red or yellow early instead of hiding the problem and trying to solve it alone. Everyone should status objectively, according to the RYG criteria, not on how he or she feels about the priority.

2. **Focus on the problems, not the people.** It is hard to encourage transparency when you are whacking the head that was transparent. People are not red. KPIs and priorities are red—or green or yellow.

When Jack first used RYG in their Weekly Adjustment Meetings, it seemed natural to ask a team member, "Hey, why are you red this week? How can we help get you back to green?" They were inadvertently shining the spotlight on the person instead of on the problem that needed to be solved. This felt very uncomfortable for Jack and his team. When I sat in on a weekly meeting, I noticed this subtlety. We shifted their questions from "Hey, why are you red?" to "Why is this priority red? What can we do to move this priority from red to green?"

---

3 Liz Wiseman, *Multipliers* (New York: HarperBusiness, 2010), cover.

Minor Majors are small shifts

or tiny changes that produce a

major change in results.

This line of questioning unfroze their brains. It helped people relax and focus on solving problems. As Jack's executive team shifted their focus from the person to the priority, they found their Weekly Adjustment Meetings to be much more productive and engaging, leading to stronger results for the company. This is a Minor Major. Minor Majors are small shifts or tiny changes that produce a major change in results.

Some companies might have to first work on their culture and the health of their teams before this kinder, gentler red-yellow-green will work for them. When we first used our dashboards at Metasys, the team did not react positively to the process. They were worried that failures would be highlighted and it would be personally embarrassing. This is natural. This response comes from self-preservation. The team's fear and worry will either dissolve or intensify based on your behavior when the dashboards show red. Will you see red, too? Or will you embrace the opportunity to manage a red priority back to green?

At Metasys, to help dissolve fear, I gave everyone a "get out of jail free card." In other words, there were no personal consequences to sharing a priority that was statused red. I wanted people to share that they needed help as quickly as possible. I wanted us to not worry about personal consequences and focus on solving problems. I have found that using the "get out of jail free card" is a good way to build this habit of self-accountability in a nonthreatening way.

Using the "get out of jail free card" is a good way to build [a] habit of self-accountability in a nonthreatening way.

I am often asked how to handle a team member if they consistently status their priorities red week after week, quarter after quarter. First, I would suggest spending time coaching and working with the team member to understand any obstacles that might be in the way of achieving the right results. Seek to understand before passing judgment. However, once it becomes clear that you do have a performance issue, I would suggest that you handle this through your Human Resources and performance-appraisal process. Don't handle this issue in a team environment or your Weekly Adjustment Meeting. Your Weekly Adjustment Meeting needs to be a safe place to work on solving problems. It is the wrong place to discuss personnel performance issues. Do continue to hold each other accountable to achieving weekly actions and quarterly priorities during your Weekly Adjustment Meeting. Continue to focus on the priority, not the person. Then have a separate performance and behavior discussion with the failing team member.

RHYTHM EXPERT TIP

Use the collective intelligence of the team. Encourage team members to share when they are stuck or off track early, allowing the team to help by discussing solutions and possible adjustments. Winning teams consist of team members that can admit mistakes, allowing them to more quickly begin discussing adjustments.

Commit to the Do Rhythm of reviewing statuses and discussing solutions weekly. Course corrections cannot happen effectively if you do not discuss your data and insights weekly. Focusing on the issues instead of the person will create a healthy team environment that will allow you to solve problems together and get stronger and better as a team.

When to Make Critical Adjustments

The University of Washington Huskies made it to the 1936 Olympics—an amazing feat. Winning the eight-oar race was miraculous.

Bob Moch, the coxswain of the Huskies crew team, was facing a sea of red flags as they climbed into their boat the day of the eight-oar final. There were an incredible number of factors *not* in their favor.

By the time the team had reached Berlin in their third-class berths, one of the Huskies, Don Hume, had taken ill. Don's position on the team, known as the stroke, was key. The stroke is responsible for taking direction from the coxswain and then setting the stroke rate for the boat. Without a strong rower in the stroke position, the team would struggle to execute its winning move. After expending precious energy to win their heat to get to the final, Don Hume looked worse than ever. Yet the team and coach had made their decision. Don was a key part of their execution plan, and he would race in the final, even if they had to carry him most of the race.

But Hume's illness was only one of their challenges. "It simply wasn't a fair boat race," Moch said. "Instead of drawing for lane assignments, we were placed in Lane 6, where the wind was blowing and the water was rough."[4] The Germans were in Lane 1 and the Italians in Lane 2, the two best-sheltered lanes. Moch was responsible for steering the boat against wind and choppy water. One wrong movement of the rudder could cost them the race.

---

4   Blaine Newnham, "Nine UW rowers who showed up Hitler in 1936 and won gold," *Seattle Times*, May 11, 2004.

The seventy-five thousand fans screaming, "Deutschland! Deutschland!" made Don's task even harder. They did not hear the race begin! The starter shot rang. The other boats lurched forward. Joe Rantz, in the seven seat, shouted, "The race has started. Let's get out of here!"[5]

Immediately, the Huskies were behind. Hume was slumped, eyes closed, mouth open, rowing but barely making it. The noise was deafening, making it almost impossible for Moch to do his critical job of setting the pace and making adjustments. As the opposing teams rowed harder, their lead over the Huskies grew. Germany and Italy were out in front. At the halfway point, the Huskies were an entire boat length behind.

As they approached the point at which they would have to begin their sprint, Moch considered a critical and risky adjustment. He could get Joe Rantz, who was right behind the barely conscious Don Hume, to set the stroke rate. But just when it was time, Don Hume woke up. Moch upped the rate, and Don began pulling for all he was worth.

But they were far behind and their usual winning stroke count wasn't going to cut it. Bob adjusted, bringing the rate higher and higher until they were at an unbelievable rate of forty-four strokes per minute. "Now! Now! Now!" he shouted into his megaphone. The crowd in the grandstands in the last two hundred meters of the race was screaming so loud that Moch thought the team couldn't hear him calling the rhythm, even with his megaphone. He started rapping on the side of the boat.

Gradually, they pulled forward. With two hundred meters to go, they were in third place. They bypassed Italy. And with just meters to the finish line, they pulled in front of Germany. History was made at the 1936 Berlin Olympics. Everything came down to the adjustments Bob Moch made in the heat of race.

....

5   Ibid.

And that is how you will win your thirteen-week race.

Adjustments are difficult. Being an aware company, observing and noticing when to make adjustments, separates companies with great execution from others. The Do Rhythm and building self-account-ability through the RYG process helps you become an aware company. Being aware is just the first step. Doing is the second! You have to look for two types of adjustments every week.

→ **Bright spots:** These are things that are working well that might be duplicated elsewhere in the company.

→ **Corrective actions:** These are the solutions to get your reds and yellows back to green.

Much of the rest of this part of the book is focused on a process to help you work on solutions to problems, to help you identify corrective actions to take when you see reds and yellows. Most leaders seem to be able to do this fairly well. What is more difficult is looking for and discovering bright spots, and replicating them across the company, resulting in huge value!

Scale Bright Spots

When I asked Don Fraynd from Chicago Public Schools about his Weekly Adjustment Meetings, he said, "I think what was really powerful for the team was to see the shining stars emerging. On more than one occasion, one principal would turn to another principal in the group whose KPIs were doing really well and say, 'Hey, what's going on? How are you pulling that off?'" And among the staff at the schools, the same thing was happening.

Each of the turnaround schools had attendance as a primary KPI. So they instituted a program that involved members of the staff. When a kid would hit a certain threshold of absences, the school would dispatch a home visitor—a teacher or a coach—to go to the home and talk to the family and the student. They were trying to find out what was keeping the student out of school, encourage them to improve their attendance, and find out how the school could help.

Each school tracked the effectiveness of those home visitors on dashboards. And when it was clear that a home visitor had a really good track record of improving attendance, the principal would ask, "What are you doing that is working? How did you achieve these results? Can we send someone to ride along with you and watch how you have the conversation?"

In fact, Don did this at quarterly meetings, too, particularly when he began leading a larger group or network of schools. "For the first day of the quarterly session, I had all of the principals who made the most progress in certain areas present what they had done the previous quarter—what their priorities were, how their top five and main thing worked. Everyone else got to choose which presentation they went to. That helped inform everybody's thinking for the next quarter."

That's how you scale the bright spots. Bright spots is a term coined by Chip and Dan Heath in *Switch*. Our human brains tend to focus on the negative. But we need to be able to spot the positive, because that's where solutions or opportunities often lie.

Bill Roberts, VP of Sales at ImageFIRST, was trying to get more sales meetings with nurses who were office managers. One day he decided to try something new. He bought a stuffed teddy bear as a gift for the office manager that he was calling on. He received the usual "She's busy and will call you back." Bill thanked the receptionist and left the teddy bear with the receptionist. He was almost to his car when the receptionist came running out of the building to let him know that the office manager had freed up and would see him immediately. After this happened a couple more times, Bill knew that this was a bright spot. In fact, Bill shared with me that he started walking back to his car slowly so that it would be easier to catch up with him! The teddy bears were working! His team discussed this as a bright spot that could scale across the sales team. Their meeting ratio went from 10 percent to 50 percent with the teddy bears!

Most CEOs seem to have more difficulty discovering bright spots. We have been taught how to notice and solve problems more than how to notice what is working well. You need to pay attention to the SuperGreens when they happen. When you see a SuperGreen status on any dashboard, slow down and ask questions to understand it. Ask questions like

→ Tell me, what is working so well for you?

→ What actions did you take that caused this potential Super-Green result?

→ What is unique about this situation that produced the Super-Green result?

Learn from the SuperGreen bright spots. There may not always be an opportunity to scale the approach to other team members or parts of the company. But sometimes there is! And you don't want to miss those times.

• • •

In the rest of part 3, we will discuss how to use a powerful Do Rhythm to make the right adjustments to beat your competition. You will learn how to *prepare* for a great week every week—the secret to having a great quarter and a great year. And you will discover how to leverage the intelligence of your team to make adjustments weekly in order to execute with speed.

....

Bottom Line

The Do Rhythm is the path to focused and aligned execution that helps you achieve your short-term plans and long-term strategies.

→ Develop a regular weekly Do Rhythm. Doing work is hard, but nothing happens until you do the work.

→ Meeting with Myself, Weekly Adjustment Meetings, and Adjustment Meetings to solve specific problems are the critical parts of the Do Rhythm.

→ The Do Rhythm helps you build self-accountability and make adjustments to keep your teams on track every quarter. Self-accountability helps you spot opportunities to make smart adjustments.

→ Use RYG success criteria and dashboards as action-oriented tools, not head-whacking clubs. To use them effectively, encourage transparency and focus on the problems, not the people.

→ Check your culture and team health. Do they promote transparency or do they promote fear of failure?

→ There are two types of adjustments: corrective actions for reds and yellows, and scaling the bright spots—the SuperGreens—across the team or company when possible.

→ Train yourself to focus on discovering bright spots.

CHAPTER 10

PREPARE TO HAVE A GREAT WEEK

Follow effective action with quiet reflection. From the quiet reflection will come even more effective action.

—Peter F. Drucker

Monday. You work hard through the week. Suddenly it's Friday. Your buddy asks you how your week was and you realize that you don't really know. You know you worked hard, very hard. But you cannot recall what you accomplished. And you know you have another mountain of work for the coming week. In your head you have a giant to-do list, and you aren't sure what items you will end up checking off. That's a tough week!

Have you had weeks like that? I have. We've all had weeks like that. But weeks like that usually do not move your priorities forward. And they do not move the company forward. Remember that this is a thirteen-week race. Every person in the company must be accountable for having a great week that pushes personal, departmental, and company priorities forward. If you are not well prepared for the week, you have already lost the battle before the week even started!

To have a great week, we all have to take a few minutes at the end of each week to review, learn, and plan for a great week next week.

Meeting with Myself

Abraham Lincoln once said, "If I had eight hours to chop down a tree, I'd spend six sharpening my axe." The Meeting with Myself is the single most important thing you can do to stop having tough weeks and start only having great weeks. Take Abraham Lincoln's advice and sharpen your axe.

At the end of every week, take some time out to briefly review the week that just ended and prepare for a great week ahead. Here are three easy steps to do that:

→ **Step 1: Identify your victories.** Review the week that just ended: How did you perform? Did you discover any insights? What were your big wins that will help you or the team achieve the plan? Status your priorities and KPIs on your dashboard: Actively look for bright spots, those activities that helped you maintain green or even SuperGreen, the ones that the rest of the team might be able to replicate or scale. Bright spots are rare, so you really have to search with purpose to notice them. If you discover one, then prepare to share and discuss it with the team.

→ **Step 2: Determine what you're accountable for.** Do you have any priorities and KPIs that are statused red or yellow? If so, come up with a corrective action plan to discuss at next week's Weekly Adjustment Meeting.

→ **Step 3: Plan for a successful next week.** Based on your review, status, and the plan for the quarter, what should your priorities be for the next week? Don't just stop at your own priorities. Consider what you need to do to help the team achieve the overall company plan. Visualize what a great week will look like. Complete the sentence "I will be successful if . . ."

I've provided a simple Meeting with Myself template to help you. You can download it at www.PatrickThean.com.

Rhythm™ Growth Tools	Meeting with Myself

Step 1: Victories - What worked well this week?

Victories & Bright Spots
1.
2.
3.

Step 2: What I am Accountable for? Status my Priorities and KPIs

Reds & Yellows with Corrective Action Plans
1.
2.
3.

Step 3: Plan for a Successful Next Week

I will be successful if: (Write a simple vision of success for your week)

My Top Priorities for the Next Week
Priorities focused on the company's theme or main thing:
1.
2.
3.
Stuck (Am I stuck on anything that needs help or discussion? Who can help?)

Figure 21. Meeting with Myself template

Asking good questions can often lead us to the right answers. Ask yourself questions as you review the week. Over time, you will develop your favorite questions. To get you going, here are some questions to help you review your week.

→ **Step 1: Identify your victories.**

- What obstacles did I overcome this week?
- How did I help another teammate this week?
- Did I move any yellows to greens this week? How did I do it?
- Do I have any SuperGreens? How did I achieve those?

→ **Step 2: Determine what you're accountable for.**

- How did I do on my priorities and KPIs? Am I on track to achieve these priorities as part of the company's overall execution plan for the quarter?
- Am I stuck on anything? Any priorities or KPIs that are red or yellow that I am not sure how to solve?
- Did I complete the action items that I had committed to this week? (I'll talk more about action items in the next chapter.)
- If I accomplished my priorities for the week, did it have the result that I was expecting? What can I learn or share from this?

→ **Step 3: Plan for a successful next week.**

- What is the company's main focus for the quarter, and what can I do to help?
- What should my own main focus be for next week?
- Based on my review and the plan for the quarter, what are the three most important things I should do next week?
- Whom do I need help from next week and who can help me?

RHYTHM EXPERT TIP

Don't be afraid to status a priority yellow or red. It is the equivalent of raising your hand in class. It alerts your team to needed discussion and possible adjustments.

Tim Johnson, VP of Operations at AvidXchange, told me, "Having to take stock of weekly victories to share with the team has been an extremely good habit to help my team focus on achieving something every week. Nobody wants to say that they didn't have any victories. You can also always tell the real victories from the fake or filler victories—you know, the ones that you make up or inflate because you didn't have any actual victories. Everyone can have a bad or unproductive week once in a while, but the Meeting with Myself minimizes the number of bad weeks that I or the members of my team have had."

Get your brain engaged and prepare for a successful week. The company that gets the most brains working wins. Research shows that at most companies around the world only 35 percent of employees are fully engaged in their work.[6] The other 65 percent are clearly less productive. Get everyone on your team engaged.

Weekly self-reviews will also accelerate a leader's development. A self-aware leader who continuously learns and improves is already on the journey of becoming a great leader. Not only will a Meeting with Myself help the entire team execute like a world-class crew team, it will also grow you as a leader.

6 Towers Watson, "2012 Global Workforce Study: Engagement at Risk," July 2012.

Research shows that at most companies around the world only 35 percent of employees are **fully engaged in their work.** The other 65 percent are clearly less productive. Get everyone on your team engaged.

Slow down, meet with yourself, and be purposeful every single week.

Everyone Is Accountable to Share Their Insights

In the next chapter, I will dive deeper into how you can turn your weekly status meetings into Weekly Adjustment Meetings. But first you have to be able to communicate the status of your priorities and KPIs to your teams. Which is why I created RYG success criteria and dashboards. They allow you to efficiently and objectively communicate statuses for priorities and KPIs. The first step is to update your thirteen-week dashboard (you might be responsible for more than one if you are the head of a department) each week based on whether each priority or KPI is in the red, yellow, or green range.

If you don't status every week, you've sacrificed your future vision. It will be very difficult to proactively make adjustments when you are not on track. Here are four tips on how to use dashboards to help you execute throughout the quarter.

Look for insights to make adjustments. Don't status just to status. Status with the intention of looking for any positive adjustments (for bright spots) or corrective adjustments. Once you have entered your status, review your dashboard. Think carefully about how the bright spots were achieved in order to help your teammates do the same. If you have reds and yellows, develop an initial corrective action plan. At the Weekly Adjustment Meeting, be open to ideas from your teammates.

Status before your Weekly Adjustment Meeting. Colin Campbell asked me for one thing he could do to get his team more focused, aligned, and accountable at Hostopia. "Status your dashboards every week before your Weekly Adjustment Meeting," I told him. "Then you can stop wasting time discussing status, and spend most of your meeting time working on solutions." Later, Colin shared that he had gained two benefits by requiring his team to do this: They cut forty-five minutes out of their executive weekly meeting and they actually solved problems every week. In addition to saving time, he saw that his team got more aligned and accountable because they started working as a team to solve problems.

I have seen this improvement at every company where executives slow down to prepare for a great week.

Status your ability to achieve your plan, not just what you achieved this week. I often say, "Status your forecast." Ask yourself how you did this week compared to what you need to achieve by the end of the thirteen-week race. This is a Minor Major. Let's use sales as an example. First, what is the success criteria? If your goal is to sell $5 million of product this quarter, then green is $5 million; let's say that red is anything less than $4 million; yellow is between red and green; and SuperGreen is anything above $5.5 million. If you statused what you actually achieved, your status would be red or yellow every week until the week you actually hit $5 million in sales. This data, while accurate, would be useless in deciding if there are any adjustments necessary to achieve your goal for the quarter.

Instead, each week, review your pipeline or other leading indicators that show whether you are on track. If your leading indicators show that you will only achieve $4.2 million, then you would status this priority yellow. You should possibly come up with corrective action in order to achieve green for the quarter. If your forecast slips into red, you should seek help from your teammates to brainstorm solutions to get the forecast back to green. Statusing your ability to achieve the plan gives you the opportunity to discuss critical adjustments to possibly get back on track before the quarter ends with a poor result. This allows you to avoid getting blindsided by train wrecks and crises.

> ## RHYTHM EXPERT TIP
>
> When your success criteria are a specific number, like a revenue target, a status based on how you are doing compared to your forecast gives you more insight. At the beginning of the quarter, project out where you anticipate being in each of the thirteen weeks. If your actual weekly numbers are close to your projections, you know you are on track to achieving your goal or achieving green.

Let the human determine and provide the status, not the machine. Some people have asked me why I don't recommend an automated system that updates the RYG status based on data in the system. It's important for you to think about your status carefully and choose your status based on what you know about the past and on your insights about what you can achieve in the next few weeks. Can you achieve the stated plan? The RYG approach triggers human intelligence; it forces you to think about whether or not you are on track, and if not, how to get back on track. Engage your brain. It's the best computer anyway!

Bottom Line

Preparation is what helps you have a great week, and it is a critical part of the Do Rhythm.

→ The Meeting with Myself allows you to review your past week and prepare to have a strong next week in just thirty minutes.

→ Status your dashboard of priorities and KPIs based on specific success criteria every week.

→ Analyze your data to discover insights that can help your team during the Weekly Adjustment Meeting. Come prepared to discuss solutions and adjustments.

→ Seek intently for bright spots to scale solutions across the company.

→ Develop corrective action plans to overcome obstacles, or be prepared to have an idea-generation session with your team to make the critical adjustments.

→ Review your victories and what you learned from the week that just ended.

→ Establish what will make you successful next week and be accountable to keeping your quarterly priorities on track.

CHAPTER 11

MAKE ADJUSTMENTS TO KEEP YOUR PLAN ON TRACK

> If the general cannot master the art of variations
> and adaptability, he will not be able to deploy
> his troops to maximum advantage despite
> understanding the five strategic considerations.
>
> —Sun Tzu, *The Art of War*
> (translated by Chen Song)

Planning requires assumptions. There is no way around it. You cannot be sure what the future holds, so you make your most educated guesses based on what you know and where you are trying to go. But to execute your plan successfully, you have to make adjustments along the way based on new insights and changing situations.

Amy Radke, chief financial officer for AvidXchange, discovered how crucial these adjustments could be when the company was rolling out AvidPay. "We made assumptions about how many current clients would buy the product and how much revenue each new client would represent. But during one of the quarters, we discovered that the volume of business was growing slower than we had anticipated."

During the Weekly Adjustment Meetings of the executive team and the sales department, the problem was discussed. Why were these KPIs yellow? What was keeping current clients from adopting the new product as fast as anticipated? After discussion over a few weeks, the teams realized that it was an issue of trust. Trusting a company to help you manage invoices effectively was one thing. Trusting a company to handle your money was something else entirely.

"Either we as a company had to figure out how to change customer behavior, or accept their behavior and change our forecast model," said Amy. "The client wanted to test us and we needed more time to earn their trust. We went through each department that touched the customer and communicated the issue. We were very dedicated to taking good care of our customers and had put many controls in place to make sure that the work we were doing for them was of the highest quality and security. What we had not done was slow down to explain this to our customers. We worked together in cross-functional teams to figure out what adjustments could be made to accelerate the trust process so clients would increase their volume of business. We put a plan in place to better educate customers on the value we were providing."

AvidXchange started training customers on the front end, sharing all the details of what they were doing, how AvidPay had been built, who the partners were, and so on, to build trust in the software, the process, and the company. This adjustment helped them execute their plan and surpass their goals.

The most crucial benefit of the Do Rhythm is that it gives you insights into where your execution plan for the quarter needs to be adjusted in order to succeed. By reviewing statuses each week, discussing solutions to problems, and making necessary adjustments, you will successfully execute your plan. It all begins with the Weekly Adjustment Meeting.

How to Run a Weekly Adjustment Meeting

I cannot overemphasize the importance of making every single week of your thirteen-week race count. The weekly Do Rhythm gets every team member focused, aligned, and accountable to winning the race. The Weekly Adjustment Meeting plays a key role. At the end of this meeting, every team member should be inspired to have a great week. Everyone should know specifically what he or she is going to do in the coming week, and understand how the week works to achieve the plan for the quarter.

The first step is to transform your weekly status meeting into a Weekly Adjustment Meeting. Moving from weekly status meetings to Weekly Adjustment Meetings is a critical shift. In most status meetings, you spend 70 to 80 percent of the time reviewing statuses. By then, your team is fairly brain-dead, yet you expect them to start brainstorming solutions. Instead, in an Adjustment Meeting, each member of the team reviews statuses ahead of time and comes prepared to

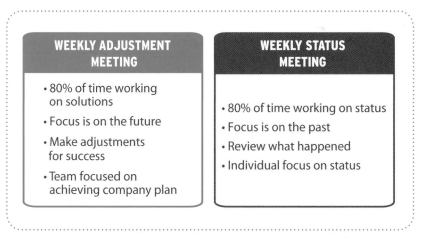

Figure 22. Weekly Adjustment Meeting comparison

Moving from weekly status meetings to **Weekly Adjustment Meetings** is a critical shift. . . . You can spend 70 to 80 percent of the time working on solutions while your brains are fresh.

engage in discussion and debate to arrive at solutions or adjustments to achieve the plan. You can spend 70 to 80 percent of the time working on solutions while your brains are fresh. This is real, productive work, not wasted meeting time.

RHYTHM EXPERT TIP

Weekly meetings should be owned by the team, not the facilitator. If the facilitator is out of the office, there should be a backup facilitator and meetings should happen without fail. It can be helpful to set your facilitation schedule for the quarter in week 1.

Develop the habit of running a Weekly Adjustment Meeting instead of a weekly status meeting. Here are some tips for running a strong Weekly Adjustment Meeting.

Appoint a facilitator. This person does not have to be the CEO or the leader of the department. Your facilitator needs to know how to run a meeting, and help the team have the right discussions.

All team members should share and review each other's dashboards and progress reports ahead of time. The best way to turn a weekly status meeting into a Weekly Adjustment Meeting is to update your dashboards or report on other metrics before the meeting, not during the meeting. Then you can spend the meeting working on solutions instead of reviewing statuses.

Come prepared with insights. Prepare by reviewing data and asking questions of your team or the people involved in a project to gain understanding and insight before the meeting.

Have an agenda with a clear objective. You can customize the following agenda to suit your team and your needs:

→ **Start with a round of good news.** Have people share their top one or two victories from the previous week. And build the health of your team by letting people share positive personal news, too.

→ **Focus on the company's plan.** Review the company's or department's dashboard—the KPIs and priorities—for the quarter. Ask, how are we doing on our thirteen-week race? What is working well? What is not working?

→ **Commit to your personal plan for the week.** Allow all team members three to five minutes to share their priorities for the week. Ask, what are you personally focused on this week? What are your priorities? How will you contribute to moving the plan forward? Where are you stuck? How can we help? Listen actively to others, and contribute any insight or advice that could be helpful.

→ **Work on solutions.** As you review and discuss the company or department plan, discuss solutions for any red or yellow priorities or KPIs.

→ **Learn from your customers.** Review specific feedback from customers. What do they like? What is working? Any requests for improvement?

→ **Commit to your action items.** During the meeting, take down action items that various team members commit to. Confirm these and have each person acknowledge and commit to the team that they will get their action items done. Capture your action items as Who What Whens (who is supposed to do what action by when). Keep the list limited to the action items that *need to get done this week.* Keep it short and keep it tight.

Don't capture a long to-do list. Focus on the key actions that are part of any adjustments to keep the plan on track. Focus on what is important.

How do you make this agenda really work for you? I have been to many weekly meetings with similar agendas. Some of those meetings were alive with meaningful discussions while others were dead. You know a dead meeting when you attend one. They are filled with presentations, statuses, and assertions. These are one-way meetings where the presenters look and feel smart and everyone else feigns paying attention. The smarter the presenter looks, the dumber the company gets. You are exhausted at the end of such meetings yet haven't accomplished much.

The smarter the presenter looks, the dumber the company gets.

A great weekly meeting looks and feels totally different. Team members come armed with data and insights. Insights to scale bright spots and corrective actions to get things back on track when they have slipped. Instead of trying to look smart, the team focuses on solutions and discovering better ways to do things. You are inspired at the end of such meetings.

Your Weekly Adjustment Meeting can run between one and a half and two hours, depending on how many discussions you need to have or solutions you need to work on. If you have only one or two key discussions, an hour and a half should be sufficient. Focus on being effective versus efficient at these meetings. Having the meeting is not the goal. Solving problems and scaling bright spots is the goal. If it takes

Instead of trying to look smart, the team focuses on solutions and discovering better ways to do things. You are inspired at the end of such meetings.

thirty extra minutes to scale a bright spot throughout the company this week, it would be thirty extra minutes well spent.

While it is important to solve what problems you can at the meeting, you also need to recognize when it's time to move beyond the meeting to dig deeper. Some problems cannot be solved by the brains in the room, or they require more information than you have at hand. You may need to set up a separate Adjustment Meeting to tackle bigger issues and establish agreement on the right adjustment.

Pay Special Attention During Weeks 4, 5, and 6

After years of following the Do Rhythm with our clients at Rhythm Systems, we have discovered a critical factor in the success of each quarter. The RYG status of your leading indicators in week four or five is critical. In the first few weeks of the quarter, it is often too soon to know how well things are progressing. In the last month of the quarter, it is often too late to make an adjustment if you're off track. The companies that succeed each quarter pay close attention in week four or five and make adjustments when there is still time to implement them. You have to be all over your dashboards and statuses at week four or five. If your leading indicators are revealing that you won't make plan for the quarter, take action immediately.

RHYTHM EXPERT TIP

If you have priorities that have not started yet by week 6, start discussing them at your Weekly Adjustment Meeting. If you get to mid-quarter and a priority hasn't been started yet, you are in danger of not achieving that priority. It's time to take action.

You do not have to wait for the Weekly Adjustment Meeting. You can schedule an Adjustment Meeting whenever you need more brains in the room to help you get unstuck. If you are not on track to achieve your goals for the quarter and have not yet figured out how to get back on track, don't wait! Schedule an Adjustment Meeting and dive in to solve your problems. Nothing happens when you wait. Get the right people together and ask what they can do differently. What adjustments can you make to get back on track? These types of regular, methodical adjustments are what will help you achieve results at the end of the quarter.

Use KPIs and Dashboards to Make Critical Adjustments

MobilityWorks is a national chain of certified wheelchair-accessible van providers. They have twenty showrooms across the country, where they offer a large selection of wheelchair vans and assistance from a staff of trained experts. MobilityWorks set an ambitious goal for growth in 2011, but early in the year, they were off track. (They knew they were off track because they were tracking both results and leading indicators.) Tracking leading indicators allowed them to make the right adjustment.

Two KPIs that supported their goal were sales appointments and the percentage of appointments kept. Sales appointments were struggling. As they explored the source of the struggle, they realized that their sales team did not have the resources to proactively call as many prospective customers as necessary to achieve the number of appointments that would lead to the level of sales they were shooting for. As they discussed this challenge, they realized that the number of outbound calls to customers was a good leading indicator to achieving their number of appointments and sales. They had to make an adjustment. Their solution was to develop a centralized call center to both handle incoming calls *and* proactively call out to prospective customers. As soon as the call center was up and running they set an aggressive priority of making thirty-four thousand outbound calls in one quarter, a priority they tracked every week on their dashboards.

This accountability to making thirty-four thousand outbound calls helped them achieve their revenue and profit targets for the year.

When you are stuck on a problem, do what MobilityWorks did. They asked questions and peeled back the onion until they found the right lever to push. This lever is often a leading indicator.

Identifying leading indicators can offer amazing insight when trying to solve a problem. Communicating and tracking that indicator with dashboards is equally important. First, it requires you to establish red-yellow-green criteria. If you are going to push on that lever to move your plan forward, how far do you need to push? Second, it allows you to get people on your team and even across departments focused on the issue. More brains looking for solutions and identifying potential adjustments is better.

Using a dashboard also helps us focus on a problem, not on a person. When you focus on a problem objectively, it is easier to face it, discuss it productively, and identify valid solutions. The dashboard is a tool that depersonalizes the problem so that you can effectively discuss, debate, and agree. It accelerates the time to solutions and adjustments because discussion of the issues is both objective and public.

If you are struggling to move your quarterly or annual plans forward week by week, review your leading indicators or find new ones that give you the visibility you need to overcome hurdles. Then track the right leading indicators on a public dashboard to move toward solutions and adjustments faster.

Using a dashboard . . . helps us focus on a problem, not on a person. When you focus on a problem objectively, it is easier to face it, discuss it productively, and identify valid solutions.

You Need a Plan B for the Big Stuff

You need a backup plan for big stuff. What do I mean by "big stuff"? That mega-important project that you cannot allow to fail. The cash-flow wall that seems to be getting closer faster! That one milestone on which all other milestones rely. You know big stuff when you see it. When big stuff is slipping into the red or even the yellow, we tend to freak out. I don't think very well when I am freaking out. Very few people do. Having a backup plan, a Plan B, for the big stuff is crucial. Develop alternative plans for the most crucial aspects of your execution when your heads are clear and you are able to consider multiple options.

When AvidXchange developed their execution plan for Avid-Pay—their key winning move—one of the critical priorities was to get virtual commercial card (VCC) payments up and running by a certain date. This was a complex process full of potential pitfalls. So they slowed down and discussed the components. What could cause the entire project to be delayed that quarter—or worse, to fail?

Michael Praeger and his team figured out that the highest-risk element was the VCC partner, a bank. What if the partner could not be ready in time? They were dealing with a large company that was not known for speed and responsiveness. In fact, this bank had already slowed them down.

"What are we waiting for? We already know that they are slow and might have trouble meeting our deadlines. So unless we are willing to punt on our revenue goals for the year, we had better have an alternative." They needed a Plan B. Critical priorities with critical deadlines *require* a Plan B.

Are you like AvidXchange? Do you have real deadlines? Most of our deadlines are not real. I mean nobody dies or goes to jail if we miss them. Oftentimes we don't even get fired. We all need real deadlines that make us sweat. A deadline is called a deadline because if you

Critical priorities with critical deadlines *require* a Plan B.

cross it, you are dead! Think about what bad things might happen if you miss the deadline. If nothing bad will happen, then it is not a real deadline. If you have real deadlines, you need a Plan B on critical-path elements to help you make the right adjustment in the heat of the moment, before it's too late. Think of Plan B as a planned adjustment at a key milestone that keeps your plan on track. Plan B is even more important when dealing with priorities that might raise team emotions. It is very hard to think when emotions are high and your brain is in a vice.

A deadline is called a deadline because if you cross it, you are dead!

AvidXchange developed a Plan B that day as part of their plan for the quarter. They spent a lot of time discussing and debating, but eventually they agreed that by a certain date, if their partner of choice was not ready to work with them on their VCC process, they would switch to a different partner. That day arrived, and AvidXchange's VCC partner was not ready. In their Weekly Adjustment Meeting, they pulled the trigger: "Let's go to Plan B." This crucial adjustment allowed their AvidPay product to be implemented on time. Not only that, their alternative partner was so happy to get their business, the terms of the agreement were more favorable for AvidXchange.

In hindsight, what was this Plan B worth? For the last half of 2012, AvidPay produced north of $600,000 in revenues. It also had a backlog of $3 million going into 2013, and it allowed AvidXchange to create a plan to achieve $5 million for 2013. If they had not made that adjustment to Plan B, they would have lost $600,000 in 2012 and several million dollars in 2013! That's what the adjustment to Plan B was worth to AvidXchange.

What about you? Hindsight is 20/20. Would a Plan B and an adjustment have saved you revenues in the past? Have you lost any revenues or clients because you were not able to make a critical adjustment? Do you need a Plan B for any "big stuff" this year?

Consider your most critical-path projects, your most important milestones, and make sure you are prepared for an adjustment if it becomes necessary.

Bottom Line

Great execution requires smart adjustments. To achieve your plans, use the Do Rhythm to explore when and how to make adjustments.

→ Meet weekly to review where you are and discuss any possible adjustments that need to be made. Turn your weekly status meeting into a Weekly Adjustment Meeting.

→ Prepare for your Weekly Adjustment Meetings by sharing the status of your priorities and KPIs with your team ahead of time. Come prepared to brainstorm, work, and solve problems.

→ Follow an agenda that keeps you focused on having the right discussions about how to scale bright spots or what action to take on reds and yellows.

→ Use Adjustment Meetings to focus on solving specific problems.

→ Pay close attention to your statuses at weeks four and five. This is the time to make adjustments if you need to.

→ When you are stuck on a problem, ask questions and peel back the onion until you discover the right lever to push. This lever is often a leading indicator.

→ Create a Plan B for any critical components of your plan so that you have an agreed-upon adjustment waiting to be implemented if the plan begins to veer off track. Be ready to pull the trigger at the appropriate Weekly Adjustment Meeting.

DO RHYTHM: 10 ACTIONS TO GET YOU DOING

1. If you haven't already, complete the Rhythm Assessment at www.PatrickThean.com.

2. Download the Do Rhythm tools, including the Meeting with Myself template and a Weekly Adjustment Meeting agenda that you can customize.

3. If you are not already having weekly meetings, establish a regular time for your team's Weekly Adjustment Meeting and get it on everybody's calendar.

4. Put your own Meeting with Myself on your calendar. Don't assume that you'll make time for it at the end of the week. If you don't plan for it, it won't happen.

5. Spend some time carefully considering accountability and the health of your team. Ask yourself, and possibly other team members, the following questions:

   → What currently happens if a project starts to go off the rails?

   → How do we deal with missed deadlines or other signs of execution problems?

   → Do we have a healthy team environment that supports collaboration?

6. If you have not done so already, publish your dashboard(s) for your team and maybe the entire company to see. Ask your team members to do this, too. Give everybody a "get out of jail free card" for the first few months of public dashboards so that they feel comfortable using the tool without fear of negative repercussions.

7. In order to identify bright spots, choose one great success story from the previous month or quarter—possibly an amazing sales number or a huge jump in productivity. Interview the person most directly responsible for it and dig deep to find out exactly how it was achieved. Next, discuss the insights you've gathered and how they might be applicable to other people or teams.

8. Set a goal to shift your weekly status meetings to Weekly Adjustment Meetings.

    First, require everybody to share RYG statuses for their priorities and KPIs with the team prior to the meeting.

    Next, ask your facilitator (don't forget to appoint one!) to use a timer during the meeting to track how much time is spent discussing statuses (what happened and why) and how much time is spent discussing solutions and how to keep moving the plan forward.

9. Consider a major struggle you are currently facing. Do you have a leading indicator attached to that issue? If not, dig deep to uncover the root of the problem and then use that insight to develop a leading indicator to help you resolve it.

10. What is the most critical deadline or milestone or deliverable your company currently has? What one thing could derail your plan? Work on developing a Plan B for that deadline that will help you achieve your overall plan.

FROM GOOD EXECUTION TO GREAT EXECUTION WITH RHYTHM

A journey of a thousand miles
must begin with a single step.

—Lao Tzu

In 2013, I was invited to speak at the ImageFIRST annual meeting in Chicago. It was a real privilege for me. As I prepared for the keynote, I thought back over the past seven years to when I first began working with ImageFIRST. I was impressed with Jeff Berstein, CEO of ImageFIRST, from our very first call. Jeff is an avid learner and was highly motivated by Jim Collins's book *Good to Great*. He was excited about taking his company on a quest from being a good company to becoming a great one. "We have a very simple business. We just do laundry for the health-care industry. I think our competitive edge has to be about being a great company. The kind of company that serves customers in a way that both employees and customers love!"

When I asked him what his biggest challenges were, he spotlighted execution. "Our business may seem simple, but it seems like it is harder to accomplish our goals than it used to be." He told me he felt as if they weren't well organized or disciplined enough. This is a problem many growth companies face, and it is easy to blame it on growth. But Jeff recognized that if the company did not get more organized and disciplined, he would still have these challenges even without growth.

As I started working with them, it was clear to me that Image-FIRST was indeed a very good company, and they were actually pretty well organized and disciplined. They had a highly talented leadership team that knew how to work well together. Yet, when their instincts told them that they needed to work on an area of the business, they did not always have confidence that they were making the right adjustments for the best results. They had opportunities to install consistent rhythms to think, plan, and do. Like our other clients, implementing these rhythms would give them a systematic way to work on their business and get the work done.

They were also missing a few leading indicators with clear success criteria that would give them insight as to where to focus their energy. For example, while they were already focused on customer service, they did not have a clear KPI to confirm that they were making impactful improvements. They had this promise on their website: "Every customer interaction will be a positive one." At our first meeting, I asked, "So how do you know if you're actually having a positive touch?" There was silence for a moment and then Jeff said, "I guess we don't." They had no way of knowing whether they were delivering on a stated promise.

Jeff understood that it would be a process and that it would take time. We started to implement the three rhythms to help him accelerate and enjoy his journey of going from good to great. And over the next five years, they were able to double the revenues of the company!

They would discover the right things to do in the Think Rhythm, build their execution plans in the Plan Rhythm, and get on a path of consistently improving their execution every week with the Do Rhythm. Over time, they grew and improved the quality of the business. On one of our coaching calls, Jeff was really excited. He said, "Patrick, my business is really simple. I have realized that if I can get every single associate at ImageFIRST to focus on four operating principles, we will become a great company: One, we need to show our customers we care and build strong loyalty. Two, our associates need to take pride in being the best they can be. Three, growth. Four, profit." I am always excited when clients tell me that their businesses are simple. That means that they have come to really understand their businesses and have found a way to explain to their employees in very simple terms where they should be focusing their energy. That is powerful! These principles eventually became known as the ImageFIRST Way. While I did not help Jeff come up with the ImageFIRST Way, we helped him roll it out by leveraging the three rhythms. Over the last seven years, this has transformed the company.

Using the Think Rhythm, they worked on the four operating principles and came up with ways to improve the company and grow their team. Using the Plan Rhythm, they planned their rollout and execution of the ImageFIRST Way over the year. They initially wanted to roll out all of the initiatives at once, but I shared with them that focusing on one at a time, developing good execution habits and consistency along the way, would improve their results in the long run. After all, the great companies did not become great overnight. They became great by improving their companies one step at a time until eventually they were great. So in the first quarter, they developed and implemented their customer loyalty programs. The quarter went well and they saw a strong improvement in loyalty metrics. They had planned to roll out programs for the associates in the second quarter. But during the quarterly planning session, as the team discussed and debated their progress, they realized that they weren't quite done with establishing the customer loyalty principle. So instead of starting a new initiative, they made an adjustment. They decided to spend another quarter emphasizing customer loyalty.

Through their second operating principle, they got serious about people. It became important to get the right people doing the right

The best companies are
able to face brutal facts
and make adjustments.

things, aligned with their strengths. They identified people who weren't doing well and then found them different seats on the bus (to use a Jim Collins phrase)—positions that would allow them to excel. We helped them identify leading indicators to focus on improving the number of A players in the company. After an initial-stage improvement, it became more difficult to increase the percentage of A players in the company. Marcus Buckingham, author of *First, Break All the Rules*, teaches that your frontline managers determine the quality and capability of your frontline employees. So we focused on the leading indicator of making sure that every manager at ImageFIRST was an A player. By relentlessly focusing on the leading indicator of "percentage of A player managers," their percentage of total A players grew by an additional 27 percent over two quarters! This was essential to executing the second principle.

The best companies are able to face brutal facts and make adjustments. As part of ImageFIRST's Think Rhythm, the executive team continually reviewed the effectiveness of the ImageFIRST Way. After two years, and much discussion, they came to the realization that while customer loyalty is key to their success, they had made a mistake in setting that as their number-one principle. Instead, they came to believe that their number-one principle should have been "Our associates need to take pride in being the best they can be." Most companies would not have had the courage to admit that mistake and make the change. Joe Geraghty, the Chief Operating Officer, led the charge as they shared this newly gained insight with all their associates and embraced this opportunity to further improve the company. I asked Joe what helped him the most to make this major rollout successful. Joe replied, "After our executive planning session, we spent time discussing this with all our different locations in their planning sessions. We asked for their input on how to best educate the associates at their locations. Everyone was excited about making associates our number-one principle moving forward."

Today, Jamee Rivers is the head of Human Resources. She provides "360" evaluations for every manager to help each one gain self-awareness as a manager and leader. Then she provides tools and training to help them grow their management skills and abilities. They have a management toolkit with fourteen specific tools that managers can use to help their associates take pride in what they do and be the best that they can be. They are serious about operating according to the ImageFIRST Way and helping people grow.

And cascading the planning process to all locations and departments got all associates focused and aligned on achieving the company's plan. Discussions about performance became team oriented and objective. This has been both empowering and uplifting for their associates, transforming them into powerful ambassadors for the company. Today, because of ImageFIRST's Customer Advocate drivers, the company receives love letters from clients who are thankful for the care their drivers have shown. Competitors may be able to duplicate their services and products, but it is almost impossible to duplicate the way they service and care for their employees and customers. This has developed into a true competitive advantage for ImageFIRST.

Jim Malandra, their Chief Financial Officer, shared that being accountable to executing their plan by using KPIs and dashboards is how they get things done now. "I am able to have good discussions every week with my team. We discuss any adjustments we may need to make. I like the idea of winning our thirteen-week race every quarter." Jeff Berstein agreed: "We have been able to make these rhythms a part of our culture quarter after quarter. They have given us a framework to be more disciplined and focused. The way the business runs now is very methodical. In some ways, despite all of our incredible growth, ImageFIRST has become a pleasantly boring place! And we are enjoying the journey of becoming a great company."

The funny thing about greatness is that as soon as you start to believe that you have achieved it, you start to decline—hubris, biting off more than you can chew, less candor and self-awareness. These are the killers of growth and greatness. Why should any company care about Think, Plan, and Do Rhythms? Because they can take you from good to great, and they encourage you to continue to learn and improve no matter what level you're at.

Why should any company care about Think, Plan, and Do Rhythms? Because they can take you from good to great.

Rhythm is a process, not an event. It takes time. You improve bit by bit by bit. Gradually you move from firefighting to fire prevention. Before you know it, you are breaking through or avoiding ceiling after ceiling of complexity. Use the Think, Plan, and Do Rhythms to get your teams focused, aligned, and accountable. Keep your plan on track as you grow your company.

Start Advancing Down Your Path Now

Start implementing rhythm somewhere. It doesn't matter where. Maybe it's KPIs or priorities or Weekly Adjustment Meetings. Yes, there is a bit of progression in the Think, Plan, Do Rhythms, but focus on making progress this week by taking a first simple step in implementing rhythm in your organization. Don't wait until you can develop an annual plan or until you've refined your list of winning moves. Start today, and step by step, you will advance down that path and your company will grow and improve.

Rhythm Resources

If you would like to download the tools discussed in this book, visit the book's website at:

www.PatrickThean.com

If you are hungry for more, you will find other resources like these at www.RhythmSystems.com:

→ Other One-Page tools to help you

→ eBooks and downloads to help you learn more

→ Meeting Facilitation Guide

HAVE PATRICK SPEAK AT YOUR NEXT EVENT

"Patrick really packs a punch! He's got so much stuff that's amazingly simple to integrate into business."
—Godvindh Jayaraman, Entrepreneurs' Organization EMP Attendee at MIT

To book a speaking engagement, contact speaking@rhythmsystems.com

RHYTHM PRODUCTS

When it comes to Breakthrough Execution, we wrote the book and built the software!

The Rhythm® Platform provides one place to help your team Think Plan Do® and achieve airtight execution.

The Rhythm® Platform includes:

→ **Cloud-based software** for executive and departmental teams

→ **Step-by-step tools** to do strategy and planning sessions

→ **Rhythm consulting experts** that will help you every step of the way

Contact us to help your company achieve Breakthrough Execution!

Learn More About Rhythm	Schedule a Meeting	View Case Studies
Call Us	See How Rhythm Works	Learn More
704 209 7290	Products@RhythmSystems.com	RhythmSystems.com

ABOUT RHYTHM SYSTEMS, INC.

Rhythm Systems, Inc. was cofounded by Patrick Thean and Cindy Praeger. Since 2007, the team at Rhythm Systems has been dedicated to helping leaders achieve their dreams, and by so doing, changing the world for the better.

Rhythm Systems provides a proven process with a clear path to help companies achieve their goals by breaking barriers and overcoming obstacles as they grow. The team achieves this by providing

→ A proven method with simple tools that inspire action;

→ Coaching that includes sharing from experience, teaching, and guiding as well as holding teams accountable to achieve their best;

→ Rhythm software that provides a platform for focus, alignment, and accountability as well as collaboration up and down and across the company.

Most clients engage with Rhythm Systems using a combination of these services and products:

→ **Rhythm:** Our patented software that provides a personalized level of coaching to help everyone on the team understand how to execute in such a way that achieves the company's plan and strategy.

→ **Facilitated Planning Sessions:** Facilitated strategy and execution planning sessions, freeing up key executives to participate fully. Our coach facilitates using questions and patterns that lead to robust discussions and good decisions.

→ **Village Coaching:** Our unique coaching process allows clients to draw from deeper experience from multiple coaches as compared to the typical single coach to a single client.

Companies who engage with Rhythm Systems experience

→ A more joyous path toward success as our coaches help them find a way to achieve results and stronger relationships at the same time.

→ A focus on an inspiring future in which their teams understand how their daily priorities connect to the company's strategy and winning moves. Everyone understands the part they play in the company's journey.

→ A repeatable process to develop compelling strategies, translate them into execution goals, and then cascade these to all departments and teams in the company.

To explore more, visit www.RhythmSystems.com.

INDEX

ABOUT THE AUTHOR

Patrick Thean is a successful serial entrepreneur who has started and exited multiple companies. As Founder and CEO of Metasys, Inc., he grew Metasys to a ranking of 151 on the Inc. 500 list.

An international speaker, Patrick has spoken to thousands of businesses in the United States, Canada, Asia, and Australia. He has spoken at

→ Numerous YPO (Young Presidents Organization) and EO (Entrepreneurs Organization) chapters

→ Fortune Growth Summits

→ National Corporate Conferences for companies such as Charles Schwab, Ingram Micro, Northwestern Mutual, and McGladrey, just to name a few

He is best known for helping companies accelerate their growth by focusing on great execution. He is exceptional at getting executive teams and their departments focused, aligned, accountable, and executing as a team to achieve their company objectives. His clients experience breakthroughs using this approach and tools that result in drama-free, accelerated growth. These tools are also part of the curriculum for the Entrepreneur Organization's world-renowned Entrepreneurs Master's Program held at MIT, where Patrick served as Program Cochair for seven years. He also chairs a similar program in Malaysia: "Taipan: The Making of Asian Giants."

Currently a Cofounder and CEO of Rhythm Systems, Patrick is the creator of Rhythm Software.

Patrick received his Masters of Engineering and Bachelors of Science in electrical engineering from Cornell University. He was named an Ernst and Young Entrepreneur of the Year for North Carolina in 1996.

Patrick enjoys digital photography. Happily married for twenty-three years, he is the proud father of two daughters: one who loves dance and the other gymnastics. Patrick supports Samaritan's Feet, a Christian charity focused on putting ten million pairs of shoes on the feet of ten million children around the world in ten years.